Catholics and Protestants:

SEPARATED BROTHERS

† / †

Catholics and Protestants:

SEPARATED BROTHERS

Léon Cristiani and Jean Rilliet

Translated from the French by
Joseph I. Holland, S.J., and Gilbert V. Tutungi, M.A.

THE NEWMAN PRESS
Westminster · Maryland
1960

Originally published in France under the title, *Catholiques, Protestants: frères pourtant,* by Librairie Arthème Fayard Paris. © F. Brouty, J. Fayard et Cie., 1954.

Imprimi potest
ABDALLAH DAGHER, s.j.
PRAEPOS. VICEPROV. PROX. ORIENT.
Beyrouth, July 8, 1959

Imprimatur
EUSTACHIUS J. SMITH
VIC. AP. BERYTEN
Beyrouth, July 11, 1960

The *Imprimi potest* and *Imprimatur* are official declarations that a book or pamphlet is free of doctrinal and moral error. No implication is contained therein that those who have granted the *Imprimi potest* and *Imprimatur* agree with the opinions expressed.

Translator's Foreword

At this critical moment of history the importance of religious unity is all too obvious. Any and all efforts to help restore this unity in a climate of Christian co-existence are worthy of prayerful study. Not only Pope John XXIII but men of all faiths should place the interests of Jesus Christ above petty quarrellings. It is precisely to repair the rent garment of Christ that works of the present nature are being undertaken. Whoever reads this book will meet rhetoric and dogma, wherein lies the seed of grace to make all see the lumen Christi. *We know that this seed, planted in ancient times, bloomed vigorously into the tree that sheltered the peoples of the world. In time many of the branches dropped, withered, but never wholly died. The watering of divine grace can resuscitate the branches to their pristine greenness and strength.*

Men of good will, such as Canon Cristiani and Pastor Rilliet, can do much to help this process along. Let men have good will; God will accomplish the rest.

Unquestionably Protestants will be tempted to side with the Protestant Pastor, as Catholics will lean toward the Catholic Canon. Yet, unity is a divine command: ". . . be one as I and the Father are One." That unity will come only from a serious re-examination of what Christ said and did. Unity in, through and by Christ is the all-important consideration.

The efforts of Pope John, the prayers of millions of religious-minded people, and the need for humility, charity, and calm scholarship should create the atmosphere for reunion. From there on one must rely on the efficacy of God's will.

The present work is an invitation to thoughtful analysis and, as such, merits the good will of readers. "To restore all things in Christ" is the admitted aim of both co-authors. May our age see this reality achieved.

Joseph I. Holland, S.J.

Contents

Introduction

BY HENRI DANIEL-ROPS

There is no worse scandal for a Christian who is concerned about his responsibility before the God who redeemed him, than that of the division of the Churches which claim Him as their own. Christ proposed unity as the sign proper to His followers. Stated in precise words, His command binds each baptized person, whatever the jurisdiction to which he belongs: "That they be one as we are one!" The dreadful discord which Christians, as a whole, manifest is an insult to the very image of the Holy Trinity. For a Catholic, it would be a frightening hypocrisy to cast upon others—the "heretics" and the "schismatics"—the exclusive responsibility for this division. On the day of judgment, "at the evening of our life," says St. John of the Cross, "it will be with respect to love that we shall be judged."

It is in those places and on those points of doctrine where Christianity must assert itself, in the face of doctrines or realities which reject it, that this scandal reaches its peak. What does the African Negro or the South American peon think when he sees rival propagandists propose to him, in the name of the same God, dogmas and rituals which are totally opposed? Quite often too he sees them wage open warfare against each other. What reason would a materialist have to renounce his principles when he sees his self-styled converters confront one another, in the name of the Spirit of Truth, in obscure contests?

*Were it only for these two reasons—and there are others—
the problem of unity presents itself to the Christianity of our
age with an urgency and a weightiness never before known.*

*However, this does not mean that, in order to handle the
problem, one need resort to a so-called defense of Christian
civilization, whose shining appearance (we know too well!)
conceals a lot of suspicious wares. The union of the children
of God cannot be realized in the bosom of a quasi-coalition
of the famous "spiritual interests" against the forces which
threaten them, even though we could without difficulty apply
the terrible warning of Christ to the present day: "If you do
not change, you will all perish."*

*It is extremely doubtful whether the needed unity could be
reconstituted through congresses, conferences or assemblies
like those in which states confront each other, or even in labo-
rious negotiations. "We think," wrote Père Daniélou very ac-
curately, "that this unity is more closely related to those deep
interior evolutions which lead to a modified stand on certain
questions, give rise to unforeseen points of contact, and cause
impediments to disappear." Each baptized person can do
much more to achieve that slow rapprochement with the
others by deepening his faith, by ever rediscovering Christ's
charity and its needs, and, in brief, by praying and worshiping.
Union cannot be realized primarily on the human level, but
by participating in the divine mystery of Unity.*

*   *   *

*Signs of this multiple effort are rather singularly numerous
in our age. We find that not one of the least paradoxes of this
century which formulates so many is to see humanity, torn in
such a variety of ways and dismembered, dream of a lost unity.
From the saintly Cardinal Mercier, the burning apostle of the
Conference of Malines, to that outstanding priest of Lyons,
Abbé Couturier, who died a year ago and to whom his friends
of all faiths have just dedicated a stirring memorial, or to that*

good Father Watson, the founder of the Franciscans of the Atonement, who founded the Octave of Christian Unity, more and more numerous are those among us who experience the agony of the great scandal. Even this Octave of Christian Unity, which, each January from one apostolic feast to another, brings together not only Catholics but many of their "separated brethren" in a self-same transport of prayer, has more than the significant value of a sign; it is already a practical realization, a claim on Providence of which there are others.

Among Catholics, the return to Holy Scripture, so evident at present, and the ardent attention conceded to the Bible are, in a sense, a rapprochement. Among Protestants, the growing surrender of a definite liberalism and the return, under the influence of Karl Barth and his school, to a dogmatic religion strongly supported by revealed truth, correspond, in another sense, to an advance toward the Catholic position. Inestimable is the debt owed to such men as Père Congar or Père Daniélou for the discussions held with the Reformed, or to Père Dumont or Père Jugie for those held with the Christians of the Orient.

The frank and fearless works of an Oscar Cullmann on Saint Peter and his role in the origin of the Church, have largely contributed in removing from Protestants of good faith certain a priori convictions which separate them from Catholics. The genuine chances of unity lie on these two levels: common prayer, and straightforward research on the points of convergence and divergence.

* * *

The present book, we are firmly convinced, will add an important element to this labor of good will. On the theme which was proposed to them, two men of God, two "separated brothers," accepted to engage in a dialogue on "Catholics and Protestants, Separated Brothers." The title which was

*suggested to them indicates in what direction they were ex-
pected to proceed. One is a Catholic priest, Canon L. Cristiani, long a professor at the Catholic Institute of Lyons, who,
throughout a life completely dedicated to the study of the history of Protestantism and Protestant doctrines, has known how
to make himself respected by his very opponents for the sound-
ness of his inquiry, the integrity of his intentions, and the
calmness of his judgment. The other is the Calvinist Pastor,
Jean Rilliet, originally from the French-speaking cantons of
Switzerland and at the present time Pastor of the French
parish of Zurich, a man of charity and apostolic zeal, whose
regular articles in the* Tribune of Geneva *have for a long time
attracted attention by the impartiality of his criticism and by
the generosity displayed in his reviews of Catholic books as
well as those of his co-religionists. The acceptance of these
two men (who did not even known each other before); better
still, the enthusiasm which they displayed in engaging in the
project proposed to them; and, at the end of it all, the friendship and esteem which they conceived for each other, are
already a testimonial. In the strongest sense of the word, this
book, born out of their collaboration, out of an exchange of
letters which brings to the driest dogmatic discussions the
warmth and liveliness of debate among friends, this book,
whose title speaks for itself, is definitely a book of good will.
What strikes one, on reading it, is the tone of deep sincerity,
of absolute sincerity which one meets here.*

*Neither one has sought to slant his opinion or to hide the
difficulties which he met on the way. Each says what he has
to say without temper, but with the clearness that the high
interests at stake demand. Neither evades the criticisms which
he considers it his right to address toward the Church to
which the other belongs. At times the tone is strained: one
feels that while formulating reservations or accusations, even
the one who writes them suffers. Yet truth has its demands
which takes precedence over all others. In this work, one is as*

far as possible from a certain climate of pretended tolerance which leads to confusions, and from that tendency to a vague syncretism where, under the pretext of smoothing over difficulties and drawing closer, one betrays what are, ultimately, the essentials of truth and faith.

However, the intention of drawing closer together, the desire of true brotherly contact is no less evident. Rising above all the differences, what Canon Cristiani and Pastor Rilliet seek to discover are, not the reasons for the conflict, but the means of union in common charity. Where does what separates us begin, and where does what unites us end? This double question is implied throughout these pages, where all the sizable problems which present themselves to Catholics and Protestants in their relations with each other are discussed in turn.

* * *

The plan followed—that of the Credo—allowed the establishment of an inventory of the problems. Since, taken as a whole, the Creed constitutes the unshakeable basis for both parties, it was expedient to follow it point by point, verse by verse, to make a complete survey of the two doctrines. What reality does each find in those sacred formulas? The real problem is there. One thinks of that axiom of Confucius: "Men would always understand one another well, if the words were always precisely defined."

It is in defining the words and in showing the precise meaning of each formula of the Creed that the two authors of this book have been consistent—a thrilling elucidation. To the impartial reader, the dominant impression received from this exchange of letters is that of an impressive concord. Taking some sentences from either one of them, one would very often feel puzzled to say whether the Catholic priest or the Calvinistic Pastor wrote them. "Truth, for us, is identified with Christ

Himself." "What is the end of creation? The possession of God in charity." "Who are the saints, if not the hearts, tilled over deeply by the Father, in which the living Word takes deeper root?" "Faith speaks louder than reason." Two of these quotations are from Pastor Rilliet; two from Canon Cristiani. Which are which? To readers who would like from the beginning to measure to what calm heights these two men knew how to elevate themselves in being joined together in mutual charity, one would advise reading the two letters which comment on the verse of the Credo: "I believe in Jesus Christ, the only Son of God, our Lord." Let us read these words which one of them has written, and which the other might just as well have written:

"If we search for that which unites Christians, whatever be the denomination to which they are attached, is it not in their communion with Christ that we shall detect it? . . . While reading these reflections on God and on the Trinity, I was considering how near what you believe is to what we believe. God is love; the miracle of Christ is to make that love accessible to us and, having made it incarnate in His brief life, to permit all men, from age to age, to know God such as He is in His eternal and inexhaustible love."

Such a book, then, bears testimony of utmost importance. Here we have a clear statement of the points on which Catholics and Protestants differ and of those on which they agree. According to the profound remark with which Canon Cristiani brings this exchange of letters to a close, the crucial point, the one to which it is necessary to draw attention and to expend most effort, is "the idea that Protestants and Catholics have of unity in truth." It is too easy to say that as long as one is in agreement on fundamental truths, one can pass over the secondary truths to draw closer together. Where do these begin and those others end? That is the Gordian knot. The Church refuses to make such distinctions between revealed truths. She adds that Protestants themselves seem to find a lot

*of difficulty in making this division, since, on points of doc-
trine as fundamental as predestination, their opinion has
changed and they have practically abandoned the ideas of
Calvin. It would, then, be of primary interest that the conversation between Canon Cristiani and Pastor Rilliet be prolonged, and that a new exchange of letters treat, henceforth,
of those truths which, although secondary in the eyes of
Protestants, are essential in the eyes of Catholics. To achieve
a further clarification of this debate, however, a second volume would be necessary.*

Catholics and Protestants:
SEPARATED BROTHERS

I

† / †

"A Sincere Confrontation"

1.

Dear Canon Cristiani,

To speak with an open heart on what unites us and what divides us, as we have planned, means incurring many risks. Oftentimes, discussion irritates the soul, and the ditch which one would like to fill up becomes deeper. Your charity undoubtedly will be put to the test many times: I live in another world than your own, and some of my judgments will seem rash, not to say blasphemous. However, I dare to hope at the beginning of our correspondence that it will manifest our unity. For the unity of Christians exists, even when they live separated by centuries of division and mountains of prejudices. Their prayers are addressed to the same God, to the same Christ. One day the occasion is offered them to come together: they speak of life and men, of heaven and prayer, and they discover with amazement how close they are. During the war, while the Swiss army was mounting guard on the frontier, I lived the long months of service as a Protestant chaplain by the side of one of your priests, a wonderful man with a magnanimous heart. We stayed in the same room, shared all our meals. We used to speak of our parishes, of the souls for which we cared; and the closeness of our reactions astonished me. On the General Staff to which we belonged, we defended the same points of view and adopted the same attitudes of mind. The same uniform made us two comrades to whom officers and soldiers alike bore the same friendly esteem. One day, the war being over, we saw each other again, he in black, and I in grey. Upon our return to civilian life, we ran the risk of being penned up, each in his own Church. I swore an oath, Reverend Canon, not to forget the harmony experienced during the course of those days when, as companions, we walked together in step beside our regiments. The memory of those bygone conversations encourages me to open up to you, just as I did some time ago to my friend; and in all simplicity and confidence, to say to you—confronting the complex problems posed by the future union of the Churches—what I believe, what I fear, what I hope. It is probable that the wall which is erected between us will not be overthrown by our correspondence, but to have exchanged our convictions over it will help us find it less high.

Kindly accept, my dear Canon, the expression of my respectful esteem in our Lord.

JEAN RILLIET

2.

Reverend and dear Pastor,
It is with deep emotion—an emotion of joy, be sincerely convinced of it—that I come to reply to your first letter.

What will be the outcome of our correspondence? On the whole, a sincere confrontation, at least, of our points of view and our convictions. We shall bring to it the same sincerity, the same frankness. I shall have no difficulty, believe me, in using formulas of peace only, or in avoiding everything that could justifiably wound your feelings. Moreover, the injuries caused by one soul to another are expressly in the intention; and our common Lord and Master, Jesus Christ, sweet and humble of heart, is my witness that never have I had, nor ever will have, the intention to hurt anyone. Our common end is truth, is it not? We are not of the company of those who say, like Pilate: "What is truth?"

We believe that it exists and that it has been brought to us. We believe, too, that we have only to apply ourselves valiantly to its pursuit in order to encounter it, even if the task requires much time, and, I shall say, even if we only touch it implicitly by our desires and our efforts.

I am very much affected by the thought that you have already lived in close relations with a Catholic priest and that you have appreciated his spirit of faith and charity as well as his zeal for souls. Meanwhile, during the course of our correspondence which will bring us wherever God will lead us, we may be able to go a lot further than you could in your first encounter.

We are definitely resolved not to avoid mentioning, on the one hand, any point of unity between us or, on the other, any point of difference. We are quite decided to throw light on every traditional object of discussion between Catholics and Protestants. Yet, what will be novel and what might have plunged our ancestors of the sixteenth century into great astonishment, is the spirit of charity, of courtesy, of righteousness, of unadulterated apostolic ambition which will animate each of us. On my part, I would dishonor the Catholic faith should I not show it, at the same time, in all its comprehension and in all its necessary and divine intransigence. What is, is. Our Lord has said: "Let your language be 'yes, yes, no, no.' " Say "yes" if it is "yes" and "no" if it is "no."

It remains true that we are fallible and imperfect creatures, and that we ought to implore in prayer that God help us in the huge task that we undertake. Without His illuminations, and despite all good human will, we shall arrive at nothing.

Kindly accept, dear Pastor, the homage of my very brotherly affection in our Lord.

L. CRISTIANI

II

† / †

The Separation

3.

Dear Canon Cristiani,

Your friendly letter is precious to me and encourages me to persevere in an undertaking which certain people judge to be useless. I myself tremble at times when I think about the judgments we make, so different for a Catholic and a Protestant, on a given fact, on a given doctrine. Luther, Zwingli and Calvin had their impassioned calumniators and their enthusiastic admirers. In the presence of these three leaders, neutrality is practically impossible. For some, they have torn asunder the Church and hurled Europe into a succession of catastrophes, of which the first was their rebellion; the second, the French Revolution; and the third, Communism. For others, their work was necessary for the safety of Christianity; they arrested the decline of piety and morals, rediscovered the way of the Bible, and prepared for the recovery of Catholicism itself. It should not be a question here of debating that trial once more. As we have agreed, we shall simply speak out in the face of the formidable crisis which we feel: you, as a Catholic priest; I, as a pastor. And since I hold the pen in hand, you will permit me to open fire.

Towards noon on October 31, 1517, a monk posts on the principal church of the fortress of Wittenberg ninety-five theses pertaining to indulgences and to the nature of penance. He will be thirty-four years of age in a few days; his gesture is not, then, that of an adolescent. Admitted to the Augustinian monastery of Erfurt at the age of twenty-two, he has even been rushed into a series of serious personal crises. Extremely scrupulous, he despairs at times of his own salvation and overwhelms himself with self-recriminations —which does not prevent his superior, Staupitz, from conferring on him the office of Sub-Prior of the monastery of Wittenberg. In their frequent conferences, the elder strives to calm the agony of mind of the younger; he points out to him in his unrest an indication of life: true penance commences with the love of justice and of God (cited by Strohl, *Luther*, 2nd edition, p. 65). Little by little the young monk finds peace; the study of the Epistle to the Romans and of St. Augustine leads him to a staggering notion of divine piety: "The Christian," he writes "knows himself always as a sinner, always justified and always penitent." This formula, often badly understood, brings together in a striking summary the humility of the Christian who recognizes himself always to be inadequate; divine grace, which casts the festive garment of pardon over the rags of the Prodigal Son—that is to say, a renewed justification; and finally the obligation for the pardoned sinner to dedicate body and soul to the service of God, who welcomes him despite his unworthiness.

I do not know what you will think of it, Reverend Canon, but it seems to be that such assertions are at the heart of the Bible. You know the rest: between this dramatic concept of the Christian and the commercial behaviour of Tetzel, seller of indulgences on a large scale, the collision is inevitable. In the Dominican to whom the Archbishop of Mayence, Albert of Hohenzollern, has confided, for a substantial commission destined to pay his debts, the charge of offering for ringing hard cash a pardon prescribed by Pope Leo X, Luther sees at one and the same time a wheedler of consciences and a skimmer of German funds. The Council of Trent in 1547, in another place, sided with the criticisms of the monk of Wittenberg (*Dict. Théol. Cath.*, Vol. 7, col. 1620).

The ninety-five theses raised a veritable tempest. Luther struck forth with some lashing formulas. The treasures of the Gospel are nets by means of which men devoted to riches were fished out before; he cries out: "The treasures of indulgences are the nets with which one now fishes out the riches of men." Against clear-cut abuses, he defends the sacred mission of the Church. Some do not pardon such an eloquent plea. Those whose interests are threatened denounce the indiscretion of the monk. Luther, when called on to retract, refuses. In the train of the incidents which you know well and which Protestant historians, like Kuhn and Strohl, relate in minute detail, the Bull *Exsurge Domine*, dated June 15, 1520, threatens Luther with excommunication. The Reformer then edits the tract *On Christian Liberty* and addresses it to Leo X, preceded by a courteous letter where he distinguishes the Pope from his following: "My heart is not turned away from Your Holiness, and I have not ceased to ask God for your prosperity and that of your Pontificate . . ." (Strohl, *op cit.*, p. 140). He would wish that his ideas be studied, placed alongside the Word of God. No! The Bull pursued its path; at Louvain, then at Cologne, the Nuntio Aleandeer had his suspect books burned. At the news of this burning episode, Luther replied on December 10 by consigning the Bull, which was accompanied by a copy of Canon Law, to the fire. He does not believe himself guilty: "I live in a renowned University, in the bosom of an approved Order," he wrote in 1519. "I make no decisions, I do nothing but raise questions; why do they call me a heretic? It is perseverance in error that constitutes a heresy" (Kuhn, *op. cit.*, p. 268). His condemnation causes him to revolt; in his turn he stands up and accuses Leo of heresy: "The die is cast; the Rubicon of schism is crossed; from now on, Christianity in the West will be divided."

Ah! Reverend dear Canon, if I recall these tragic events, it is only that they are on the horizon of our combined writings. Your fathers in the Faith have lived in obedience to Rome; mine have followed Luther and those who, in Switzerland and in France, echoed his decision—Zwingli, Oecolampadius, Wyttenbach, Haller, Bucer, Varel and Calvin, to name only a few of them. The cities and the kings choose; their decision determines the future of generations. You were born in one Church, and I in another. When I reread the annals of this extraordinary epoch, I find therein the tumult and the brutal collision typical of all revolutions. Let there be no question here of reopening bygone records. You know my convictions: I am a *Protestant*; * until I am better informed, I, therefore, believe that Luther could not have acted otherwise. You hold the opposite opinion, and that is your right. What troubles me, beyond expression, is the thought of the extraordinary burden which the three years from 1517 to 1520 have laid upon Christianity. After the brief discussions which precede the separation, there follow the long ages of independent existence. You have your customs, your rituals, your dogmas; we have ours. For a long time, even the principle *"cuius regio, eius religio"* ("every prince to his own religion") impeded all communication, all exchange. At Geneva, at Zurich, there did

* The word "Protestant" dates from the Second Diet of Speyer, which had taken severe measures against the partisans of Luther. On April 29, 1529, six princes and fourteen cities protested against this decision.

not remain a single Catholic; at Lyons, Protestantism was proscribed. The nineteenth century brings the members of the two confessions in frequent contact. Liberty of conscience and liberty of establishment destroy secular barriers. In my country, there is not an important city which does not have an active confessional minority. At Lucerne, the fortress of Swiss Catholicism, the Protestants today form one-quarter of the population; at Zurich, the city of Zwingli, the Catholics number more than a hundred thousand. Some relations have been restored; some ties have been created. Is it necessary to recall here the friendship which united the Genevan Pastor François Naville to the Franciscan Friar of Fribourg, Grégoire Girard, during the first part of the last century? Or again, that of Ernest Naville, François' son, with Père Gratry? Theologians and exegetes exchange their works today and lend the mutual support of their knowledge to the study of the Bible. We can correspond in complete freedom. From time to time, the memory of the frightful quarrel is blurred to a point where unity in conversation and in friendly exchange of views is restored. Still if on the spiritual plane communication is established, nothing is yet settled on the plane of ecclesiastical institutions; and, to tell you what I am really thinking, the enticement of a settlement does not even appear. We are still in the sixteenth century. That point must be made, if only to avoid any generous illusions. This extraordinary and contradictory state constrains us to measure the weakness of men, their inability to imagine the means of a reconciliation. It casts us back on the promise of Christ: "To men, that is impossible; but to God, all is possible" (Matt. 19:26).

But I am abusing your patience, my dear Canon; my pen runs over the paper in haste to define the spiritual situation referred to by the expression "separated brothers," which generalizes a growing mutual esteem. I rejoice in the ex-

pectation of knowing your feeling on this subject; and I beg
of you to accept, meanwhile, the expression of my fraternal
esteem.

JEAN RILLIET

4.

Reverend and dear Pastor,
Your letter of this morning plunges us into the history of
the sixteenth century. It brings back to my mind some personal memories which you will allow me to conjure up,
because that leads us straight to the facts themselves, which
you place on the first rung of the causes that brought about
the unhappy break of Christianity more than four centuries
ago.

On May 27, 1911, before the Faculty of Letters in the
University of Clermont-Ferrand, I upheld a thesis for my
Doctorate in Letters. That thesis—the main one, for there
were two—had as its title *The Evolution of Luther from
1517 to 1528*. It began, then, exactly on that date of October
31, 1517, whence your exposition proceeds. Without entering
here into the details of my thesis, which followed the foot-
steps of Luther almost day by day from 1517 to 1528, I
believe I am following your desire by summarizing the essential points of it.

In my opinion, there were three stages in the evolution of
Luther.

In the beginning, he does not yet know where he is going.
He is not unaware that his personal theology differs from
current theology. He has made a discovery which he believes

to be the exact translation of the thought of Saint Paul in his Epistle to the Romans—namely, that original sin has corrupted human nature entirely; that this nature has become sin in all that it is and in all that it does; that, in addition, it is completely stripped of free will, and even of all spiritual understanding.

In his commentary on the Epistle to the Romans, written in the year 1515–1516, he gives the following definition of original sin:

"Original sin is the privation of all rectitude and of all vigor in our physical and mental powers, external and internal; it is the leaning towards evil, the distaste for good, the boredom with illumination and wisdom, the love of error and gloom, the flight from and the detestation of good works, the promptness to do evil" (V. Scheel, *Dokumente zu Luthers Entwicklung*, 1911, no. 273).

Happily God saves whom He wills, by means of gratuitous predestination. Those whom He refuses to save are irremediably lost. Those whom He elevates out of pity receive from Him, without merit and without active intervention on their part, a marvelous gift—Faith. And they are justified by Faith without good works. Such, roughly, is his discovery which comforted his heart. He nourishes the ambition of transmitting to the whole Church the secret of salvation of which he believes he has become the privileged depositary. He reasons, while waiting for his ideas to triumph, that he will be allowed the liberty, at Wittenberg, to propose a theory which seems to be so comforting. He especially hopes that the authorities will imitate his zeal in going back beyond the Middle Ages—during which time, according to him, Christianity was scandalously secularized, made worldly, pelagianized—to the pure source of religious truth; that is to say, to the Gospels and St. Paul: in a word, to the Bible.

He is shocked by the first opposition he meets, following his brilliant exploit of October 21, 1517, the posting of the ninety-five theses on indulgences, which represent only a small, a very small, part of his main thought. This opposition he ascribes to ignorance, to the fanaticism of the School, and to the spirit of domination on the part of Rome.

As long as ecclesiastical authority, faithful to its habit of temporizing but obdurate in the matter of doctrine, crowds him (at first, through the gentle Cajetan or through the trifling Miltiz—a type of the worldly diplomat of that time—then by means of a solemn Bull, and even through the voice of the young Emperor Charles V) to make him retract his errors, Luther with loud cries demands a discussion, putting in argumentation a confidence which comes to him from Scripture, such as he understands it. He does not cease to consolidate his position. When, at the Diet of Worms in 1521, he refuses to retract, a long time has already elapsed, since, in his heart, he has broken with the Catholic Church.

From 1517 to 1519, in truth, he was able to believe that he was upholding an opinion which was temerarious perhaps, but whose existence should at least be tolerated. He no longer holds any illusion after the Dispute of Leipzig in 1519. From 1519 to 1520 his break with Rome is accomplished and affirmed in his three famous works: *The Manifesto to the Christian Nobility of Germany*, where he proclaims universal priesthood and abolishes the hierarchy; *About the Babylonian Captivity*, where he commences with the sacraments, reduces their number from seven to three, and makes their efficacy depend solely on the faith of him who receives them; finally, the *Treatise on the Liberty of the Christian*, which presents the ideal of a new religion, without authority and without a visible Church, but with total spontaneity and brotherliness and liberty and equality, but likewise without free will; and all of that realized in us without cooperation on our part, by means of faith through the Holy Spirit.

Such is the first part of my thesis. The second part pointed

out strange changes in Luther. In this part he is frightened
by the innovations which are taking place in the very bosom
of his church of Wittenberg, while he is penned up at Wartburg. Impatiently he sees a Karlstadt, a Zwilling, then a
Thomas Munzer sanction bold reforms in the name of the
Bible wielded by himself. He leaves Wartburg, in spite of
the ban of the Empire which affects him. He returns to
Wittenberg, takes over the administration, stands up bit-
terly to the revolutionaries of Karlstadt and especially to
Munzer, and hastens a return to ecclesiastical institutions,
no less rigid than those of the Catholic Church, and finally
puts all these institutions under the authority of the State.

The conclusion of my thesis was that Luther had ended
in a contradiction. This expression is not mine, but that of
Harnack, the celebrated Lutheran historian. And I cited
these words from the same Harnack:

"Once the principle is admitted according to which doctrine is, even for the Protestant Churches, a thing stopped
once and for all, Protestantism threatens to become a miserable double for Catholicism . . . miserable, for there are at
least two things which it is unable to realize, the pope and
the priest. Neither the letter of the Bible, nor the confessions of faith, nor the symbols—let us add—nor the threats
of repression by the State, can give to Protestantism that
absolute authority which the pope represents for Catholics;
and as for the priest, Protestantism does not know how to
go back to him. It remains faithful to the two principles of
the State Church and of the marriage of priests. Neither one
nor the other will set it up in good shape before Catholicism, come the day when it would like to compete with it
on this point" (Harnack, *L'Essence du Christianisme*, p.
349).

Such was the evolution of Luther. That is what led us,
on the one hand, to the Reformed Catholicity of Trent,
whose history I have told in Volume XVII of *L'Histoire de*

l'Eglise by Martin-Fliche, and, on the other hand, to what one is, indeed, forced to call multiplication—I was going to say to the rapid multiplication of churches and sects on the Protestant side. This multiplication, which Bossuet called "the variations of the Protestant Church," is considered from the Catholic angle a proof of impotence in the face of Catholic truth. Either one is unable to grasp it, or, if one does grasp it one day, it is only to lose it the next.

Yet I would not like to stress this small appearance of things. It would be simply distressing, if it had not been the occasion of so much bloodshedding, of so many hatreds, of so many unappeased spites!

What I would also like to say, pertinent to your letter, is that, in the matter of truth, as you yourself write, Luther, with his ideas and his passions, with his fighter's temperament and the secret mysticism which he cradled in his heart, could no longer submit, could no longer return to the Church of his childhood. He would prefer to resign himself to the State, with the mental reservation, undoubtedly, that the State would never do anything without him in a matter where he was the only competent authority, acknowledged as such among his own—to wit, in *Chrsitianity* based upon the Bible.

What, then, was lacking in Luther to be able to submit? You have said that he discovered a new formula: "The Christian knows himself always as a sinner, always justified and always penitent." And you add: "This formula, often badly understood, brings together in a striking summary the humility of the Christian who recognizes himself always to be inadequate; divine grace, which casts the festive garment of pardon over the rags of the Prodigal Son—that is to say, a renewed justification; and finally the obligation for the pardoned sinner to dedicate body and soul to the service of God, who welcomes him despite his unworthiness."

Your translation of the sentiments of Luther is, if I dare

say it, a translation which brings him back to Catholicism. As for Luther, humility consists in knowing oneself to be, not "inadequate," but rather totally corrupt, rotten, powerless, stripped of all rectitude and of all spiritual power. As regards the obligation of the pardoned sinner to dedicate himself body and soul to the service of God, there can be no question here of "obligation," where there is only "enslaved will." Everything takes place under the impulsion of the Holy Spirit, in such a way that humility of abjection, according to Luther, changes into arrogance because of the presence in him of the Holy Spirit, who does not permit him to bow down before the Church!

And thus we come to the nub of our fraternal debate.

To whom did our Lord promise infallibility? To the Christian, alone, isolated, as he reads the Bible? Or to His Church, the depository of the Bible?

If Luther was condemned, it was not for having disturbed certain interests, for having upset some practices, for having put an end to some complacent, tranquil moods; it was not even for having denounced some abuses, which were gross and which all of us declare we hold in abhorrence, but for having attacked doctrine, for having changed the idea of God, of Jesus Christ, His work on earth, the sacraments instituted by Him; in a word, for having meddled with the doctrine of justification, of salvation, and of sanctity.

We would never end, if we stopped at such and such a detail of history. What we must do—do you not think so, my dear Pastor?—is to rise above the dust of the facts, while keeping before us only the lessons of prudence and mutual understanding that they impose upon us. However, it will be more important to soar upwards into the heights, to contemplate God in His being, in His creation, in the tremendous Incarnation, in the wonderful revelation of the Gospel, in the formation of a Church which would become a school of saints for the elite, for the just and the penitents, and for the most simple of souls. It is without doubt in that direction that we have the greatest chances of finding a meeting ground.

On that note, I beg of you to accept, my dear Pastor, the witness of my most fraternal sentiments in our Lord.

L. CRISTIANI

III

† / †

The Principles of Protestantism

5.

Dear Canon Cristiani,
Your letter reached me yesterday, and I must thank you for the clarity with which you take a stand on the subject of Luther. Your ideas of the man, of his efforts and his revolt, are contrary to mine. You have defined him as an extremist in theological matters, led by an exaggerated pessimism to deny free will and the possibility of good works. I see him—with, I dare say, all my Church—as the courageous wrestler who takes a serious view of the abuses of his century and who, checked in his attempt at reform and begged to retract criticisms which he deems true, ends in the "I cannot do otherwise" of Worms, in spite of the risk of the stake.

I said to you that my intention was not to plead once more the trial in which you have defended with authority the Catholic thesis, just as my former professor of Strasbourg, Dean Strohl, defended the Protestant thesis in his two admirable books: *On the Religious Evolution of Luther up to 1515* and *The Expanding of the Religious Thought of Luther from 1515 to 1520* (Strasbourg, 1922 and 1924). Our correspondence shows that we remain opposed on this point —you, as a faithful Catholic; I, as a good Protestant.

There are, however, some remarks in your interpertation which go beyond the problem of Luther and which lead us into full confessional reality. You find that I give a Catholic translation to his doctrine. I do not believe, however, that I have betrayed him—*traductore, traditore* ("the translator is a traitor"). The formula which I borrow from the biography by Strohl leads to the heart of the Lutheran experience, wherein the theologian affirms the essence of his faith, aside from controversy.

Thus, we do not judge St. Augustine on the terrifying theory of predestination which he hammered out during his struggle with Pelagius. When he says, "Our heart is restless until it rests in thee," we hail him respectfully and we place him unhesitatingly in the ranks of the great believers, with St. Paul, St. John Chrysostom, Calvin, Pascal, Zinzendorf.

Supposing, just the same, that I have betrayed Luther and that I draw him toward Catholicism, because I may be consciously or unconsciously more Catholic than he, that would not frighten me. For us Protestants the distant benefit of the sixteenth century's frightful crisis of learning was to distinguish the Bible from its ever human representatives. Was it not Alexander Vinet, the philosopher from Lausanne, who wrote little more than a century ago: "Protestantism for me is only a point of departure; my religion is beyond. I could, as a Protestant, have some Catholic opinions, and who knows if I don't have some? What I reject absolutely is authority!" If a Protestant esteems as exaggerated such a declaration of the Reformers, if he believes that Luther or Calvin has badly understood Holy Scripture, he can, at his own risk and danger, adopt another position. We believe in the fallibility of individuals and of ecclesiastical bodies in the assimilation of truth. "Each witness of Christ reflects it, we think, through his personality, in the relationship of his temperament and that of his age." Sometimes he exaggerates, or he hardens an aspect of the eternal message. These variations which Bossuet makes fun of, we value as inherent to the nature of Christianity: God delivers His Son to men; He permits Him to advance among them without protection, strong in His holiness alone. It is normal, it is inevitable, that sinners, such as we are, should pull Jesus now to one side, now to another. But His Voice continues to speak. What one understood badly, another understands better. One generation arises which corrects the preceding, and in each epoch itself all the aspects of truth find their representatives. It is, in our opinion, the peculiarity of the Church that unity is born of diversity, because Christ works ceaselessly in men of good will. Far from fearing differences, we consider them as a richness from God. In this sense the Constitution of the Church at Geneva, into which I was born, lays as the foundation of its teaching "The Bible freely studied," and obliges each of its members to form himself according to personal and well-thought-out convictions. Setting out with this concept of truth, "it recognizes for its only leader Jesus Christ, Saviour of men."

Thus, we do not make of Luther or of Calvin infallible authorities; like the apostles of old, they were the servants of God, progressing slowly in the Faith, committing mistakes about which their Master often had to say, "You do not know by what spirit you are animated." No doubt you are acquainted with the expiatory monument erected by the Genevan people in 1903 on the site where, through Calvin's fault, Michael Servet perished at the stake, a formidable heretic who died exclaiming: "Jesus, Son of the Eternal God, have pity on me." (See Williston Walcker, *Jean Calvin*, Geneva, 1909, pp. 367–368.)

These propositions will probably seem to you terribly bold. I must present to you Protestantism without any palliative, in what it possesses of mad sublimity. For it needs extraordinary rashness and a very great confidence in God to believe that truth, once cast into the world, will defend itself through itself and through its own intrinsic authority, and that it will conquer. Is it not Bossuet—an unexpected ally of my thesis—who made this statement which is so proximate to mine? "If holy truth were not contradicted, we would not see the wonder that has made it last among so many contradictions, and we would forget at the end that we are saved by grace" (*Discours sur l'histoire universelle*, chap. 33). Not only does Protestantism admit exterior contradiction with liberty of conscience, but even in the very interior of Faith it applies the principle to the extreme: "*In necessariis unitas, in non-necessariis libertas, in utriusque caritas.*" It is Saint Chrysostom, a well-informed teacher, who wrote in his *Homily on Heresies*: "In the same way as the oaks, shaken in every way by the furious winds, only become stronger and put forth deeper roots when they first have taken a good direction, in the same way souls which are rooted in the true Faith, rather than letting themselves be carried off by the violent breath of heresies, grow and strengthen themselves under their blows." I shall not make of the illustrious Bishop of Constantinople a Protestant literally—that would be going too far—but that holy man had already understood in the fifth century what the nineteenth century relearned: namely, that truth need not fear a climate of liberty. Is it not also he, wiser than St. Augustine, who so nobly took a position against all violence in religious matters and dared to write: "It is not necessary to put the heretics to death; otherwise, one might start a war without mercy in the world"; and again, concerning the parable of the weeds: "Who knows whether a part of these weeds will not change into good wheat? If, then, you should pull them out at the present time, you would harm the coming harvest by tearing up those who could change and become better" (Homily 46 on St. Matthew).

We adopt this measure as far as possible, forbidding over-zealous Christians to excommunicate those who do not seem to them to be believers of good quality, leaving the wheat to grow in the field, mingled with the bad weeds, without any protection except that of the Holy Spirit, under God's sun. There is a choice for them: that of ripening. Some souls stray from the right path; they are delighted with the night. Others advance little by little from light to light. Still others, coming back from their wanderings, admit a certain certitude, a certain discipline which they had cast off. Because of this extraordinary boldness, our Churches might have died; they exist today despite four centuries of varied vicissitudes. In Switzerland, in France, in Germany, and in the extensive Anglo-Saxon world, they are instruments of Jesus Christ and even bring many souls to salvation. Is it not proved that this method has good in it, even on the political level, when Communism is rejected by a free and unanimous England, which also freely preserves its Church united to the State, its secular customs, its pious dynasties of constitutional rulers, just as in the Scandinavian countries?

If liberty has not destroyed us, as many prophesied, that is because it is a liberty with Jesus Christ. Liberty alone is an empty form; it has no life, but is a manner of living. The voice of Christ resounds as well in our Churches as in our catechisms, and some souls turn towards Him to receive the nourishing bread from His hands. In this regard—and perhaps this reality escapes the outside observer—one must perceive all that is done by Christ and for Christ in our families, in our youth groups and in our Sunday schools. There is not one of our catechumens who has not been placed in contact with his Saviour by Sacred History and by the study of the New Testament; not one of our families which does not receive a Bible the day on which it is established before God. Thus a race of believers is born: mothers who pray, fathers who watch, saintly girls who busy themselves with their nephews and nieces. The disputes of theologians are surface waves; the deep reality of the Church is placed in a sphere which is at once personal and pertinent to the family, where the speculations of brilliant minds have little significance. There, through the actions of believers on believers and through the devoted ministration of ordinary pastors of the parish, the Church lives and renews itself continually. In his recent book, *Pensée de la Réforme* (Delachaux et Niestle), Strohl speaks very justly of an apostolic succession of the faithful (p. 174). Faith is transmitted from mouth to mouth, from heart to heart. By each of its members, the living body which is the Church extends across the centuries—and that, in the climate of liberty which I have described.

The analysis of our formal principle leads me thus to faith in the Father, the Son and the Holy Spirit, in the name of whom our children are baptized. As you state so rightly at the end of your letter, it is there that in the diversity of our judgment of history we find ourselves united. The contrary nature of our ecclesiastical principles does not prevent us from discovering for each other our salvation in the revelation and action of our thrice Holy God. I rejoice that we shall take up our talk after your response to this letter, and, while waiting, I remain yours, fraternally devoted in our Lord.

JEAN RILLIET

6.

Reverend and dear Pastor,
I thought that we were going to place ourselves without delay on the terrain of our common articles of the *Credo*. Yet I shall follow you first, very willingly, on the ecclesiological terrain, although I consider, and I shall say immediately why, that we cannot settle the debate on the nature of the Church for the moment.

With much clarity you have exposed your viewpoint, the actual Protestant one. It is altogether different from the viewpoint of a Calvin or a Luther, both of whom showed themselves savage—excuse this expression which seems justifiable to me—on the question of orthodoxy and did not admit that anyone could think otherwise than they.

At heart, you are one with the opinion of Harnack in the citation which I took from him in my last letter. If he fears that Protestantism is only the "miserable doubling for Catholicism," it is that he speaks of a Protestantism in which an orthodoxy would be imposed by the State, even in the name of the Bible, as was so long the case in Protestant Europe.

In the same work from which I quoted, *L'essence du Christianisme*, he writes some pages of which I shall cite only the gist: " 'You are divided,' " he wrote, " '*tot capita, tot sensus!* (as many opinions as heads)!' Behold their objection to us! 'So what?' we reply; 'so much the better! We desire still more personal opinions, still more sentiments, different from one another, still less conformity . . . !' "

I have known that same opinion for a long time now. Pardon a man of my age who is always ready to return to his early memories. Yet you are going to see me return to our exposition straightway.

The recollection that I am going to summon up is related again to my defense of the thesis of 1911.

A professor of the Sorbonne, Ernest Denis, a well-known historian, happened to be among the members of the jury. When his time to speak came, he expressed himself somewhat as follows:

"Let us leave aside, Reverend Father, the scholastic appearance of an examination. You are a Catholic priest. I am a Protestant by birth and by religion. We are going to discuss, man to man. You maintain in your thesis that Luther ended in a contradiction because he had begun as a man of liberty and then finished by opposing a religion of liberty in favor of State religion.

"I agree with you on all that. I shall even agree that Luther was, according to his own expression, a churlish Saxon: 'rusticus Saxo'! However, that does not prevent me from hailing him, and from venerating in him the man who opened the breach by which liberty has passed on.

" 'How is that?' say you. Well, it is like this. In the traditional Catholic religion, the more pious, zealous, competent and well-versed in theology and canon law a prelate is, the more he is inclined to use his cross as a shepherd's crook to lead wandering sheep into what he thinks is the right path. As a consequence, the more pious he is, the more zealous, the more instructed and holy, according to the norms of holiness as you understand them, the more tyrannical he is over consciences, the more oppressive he is over individuals, the less does one breathe the air of liberty!

"On the contrary, with Luther, one has only to deal with the State! 'That is absurd,' say you. And you are right. But precisely because it is absurd and because the prince is incompetent and often rather lukewarm himself in the matter of piety and zeal for souls; and again, because of the numberless political worries which seize him as chief of State (such as finances, diplomacy, war, and so on), for all these reasons, it quickly happens—if one sets apart some rare 'Sacristan Kings'—that he leaves the bridle on the neck of his subjects. Provided they conform to the general rules of public order, he lets them believe what they would, perhaps in secret at first, but very soon in public as well.

"It is then by this gate that liberty has entered, and it is for that that we are grateful to Luther. He is for us Protestants a force of nature—a brute force, if you wish; blind, if you wish—but who entered the ranks at the propitious moment to bring us what we prize above all: liberty of thought, liberty of conscience, liberty of the cult of religious worship."

Such, substantially, was the discourse of Mr. Ernest Denis, and he seems to me to have expressed feelingly the same thesis which your last letter contains.

What, then, will be the Catholic viewpoint on so grave a question?

I shall say, in the first place, that we evidently do not have the same scale of values, you Protestants and we Catholics. For you, liberty is the prime consideration. For us, truth surpasses everything else.

The difference is perceptible. It is even boundless, infinite. Truly, liberty, in our eyes, is only a means and not an end in itself! What matters my possessing liberty, if it is liberty to commit suicide? Liberty was given to men only for an end which is superior to it, and which we must search for in our cordial conversations. From now onwards, I believe I can say that one of the essential ends towards which liberty tends is *truth*. What are we doing at this moment, both of us, if not *freely seeking the truth*?

I said at the beginning of this letter that I would explain why I do not believe we could settle our debate at this point.

Why? The time has come to state the reason.

We are discussing together the Protestant and the Catholic ways of understanding. But, on the fact of Christianity, is it a question of our personal ways of understanding, of our individual sentiments, of our reasonings themselves? Christianity, in truth, is not a human invention, it is not a discovery made by a thinker, by a saint, by a mystic, or by a man of genius. It is the revelation of the God-Man. We must take Him such as He is, and not such as we desire Him. That is why, after my last letter, I invited you to ascend to the topmost considerations, to rise upwards with me to God Himself by examining our *Credo*. If I follow you today on ecclesiological ground, it is because we are able to clear the terrain in a fashion, and circumscribe the sector where our differences lie. But it is not what we think, once again, that is important; it is what Jesus thought, what He said, what He wanted.

Can I believe, like the Protestants (whose thesis Ernest Denis exposed before me on the day of my doctoral defense), that He professed an eclectic philosophy, in virtue of which truth will be formed from the thousand facets of particular opinions, different and even contradictory, in such a way that no one possesses it completely unless he is God, who smiles equally and with the same complaisance on "orthodox" and "heretic"—perhaps with a predilection for the latter?

Like you, Reverend dear Pastor—and I dare say more than you, since I am your elder by far—I have searched the Bible closely, and especially the Holy Gospels. I do not yet cease to do so every day, and practically every hour of the day. I have not come across so "comprehensive" a philosophy in it; that is to say, to the point of admitting contradictions with impartiality!

Let us not hurry to conclude. Let us climb back to the heights, as we resolved to do: God, Creation, the Incarnation, the Redemption, the Church of Christ.

When we have established the "line"—that is to say, what

is in harmony with God as He has revealed Himself in the Gospels, and with Christ as He has taught us to seek Him and to meet Him—then, undoubtedly, it will seem possible to touch upon serious disagreements which separate us: liberty or authority.

As of now, however, I would like to recall a great saying of Christ, one of His profound sayings, which may clash with our human prejudices, but which possesses a divine resonance: "The truth will make you free!" (John 8:32).

You recall, I am sure, and very well, the circumstances in which Jesus pronounced this sentence. He was arguing with the Pharisees. They were proud to be "free," and they based this freedom on the sole fact of being "children of Abraham," just as in our days, one bases it on the power of thinking and of saying what one wishes. And Jesus said to them: "If you abide in My word, you will be truly my disciples, and you will know the truth and the truth will make you free."

According to our common Master, Jesus Christ, it is then truth which gives us freedom, and not freedom which gives truth of itself. Truth makes us free from error, from lying, from human opinions, free in regard to ourselves, to the devil and the world!

But let us not anticipate. We shall take up that discussion when we shall have descended the chain of certitudes and rediscovered the foundation of the Church of Christ. We shall have to ask ourselves then what He meant, what He did, what our Fathers in the Faith received from Him, and what they have transmitted to us.

While waiting, if there is a danger that we ought to dread, it is that of bending Christian institutions to the parliamentary practices of our political assemblies. In those there is need of discussion, need of total freedom of thought and word. Of those it is permitted to say that truth is made of a complexity of different opinions, indeed contradictory. All in them is relative; there is no question of the absolute.

You have cited, Reverend dear Pastor, an axiom which is, I believe, from St. Augustine: *"In necessariis unitas, in dubiis libertas, in omnibus caritas."* ("In necessary matters, unity; in doubtful ones, freedom; in everything, charity.")

That axiom, we also cite often, and we admit it in all its parts. Yet the delicate point, not for us Catholics, but for you Protestants, is to draw up the list of the *necessariis*. You also admit, then, that there is need of a definite unity, that it ought to assert itself in necessary matters, and that, as a consequence, there exists an imposing orthodoxy, at least in these matters. But what are they? That is what the Hegelian philosophy of identity or of the complementarity of contraries makes difficult to define. And yet kindly accept, my dear Pastor, the certitude that, in any case, I would not like to fail on this last term: *"in omnibus caritas."* My next letter will say why.

L. CRISTIANI

IV

† / †

The Credo: "I Believe in God"

7.

Dear Canon Cristiani,

Just as we stated, it is to the study of the Credo that our correspondence will consecrate itself. A document going back to the opening centuries of Christianity, it summarizes the convictions of the baptized. We shall comment on it, you as a Catholic, I as a Protestant, and our unity will appear from the very divergence of our views.

The Credo says "I believe." It is both a starting point and a destination. Through it, the voice of past generations is guiding me; by it, I give witness to the supernatural realities which permeate my existence. If there be Christians who recoil before this or that declaration, I shall not cast a stone at them. Jesus Christ did not set aside anyone, and his disciples understood this, only little by little, though all the while loving Him sincerely. (See Mark 4:40; Luke 24:25.) By what right shall I, who was slow to believe and to obey, repel one who is progressing step by step in the Faith?

Our first consideration, God!

If history and the judgment brought to bear upon it may divide us, it is sufficient to cast a look upon the present for the elements of unity to appear. In the face of militant atheism, or indifference, we are defending the same cause. Rather simple people translate that unity by saying: "Do we not have the same God?" or better: "They are believers like ourselves." I know of some ecclesiastics who have been scandalized by such remarks. They smell here, at times, a danger of syncretism—a compromise on religious matters—sometimes a lessening of the Faith which is reduced to a vague deism. Indeed, the affirmation of belief in the same God corresponds sometimes to this trivial minimum by which half-Christians hope to hold on to Him, for fear that a more definite conviction will impel them towards accrued moral and spiritual demands. But the declaration "We have the same God" expresses also the conviction of a sacred bond between believers of different origins.

Calvin begins the first chapter of his authoritative *Institution of the Christian Religion* with this assertion: "Nearly the whole sum of our wisdom is found in two parts: that by knowing God we know ourselves." This knowledge of God is not to be confused with a cold certitude. "We shall not say that God is known where there is no religion, no piety." Are we not fairly akin to St. Louis writing to his son: "The first truth to be grasped is to set your heart on loving God; for without that, no one can be saved." The two illustrious Frenchmen, one from the thirteenth and the other from the sixteenth century, acknowledge the same fervor. One sets out on a Crusade; the other leaves the books he loves and dedicates himself to the difficult task of making Geneva the City-Church depicted by Georges Goyau. It may be that on such and such a point their zeal appears excessive to us; their careers do not render less witness to the God they serve through it.

In deciding to go toward the unknown and the difficult, the Christian expresses his submission. Beyond his own life, himself and his personal desires, he hails the presence of the Almighty, who is reclaiming him. In the history of Protestantism you find innumerable vocations which are of the same nature as that of St. Francis of Assisi or St. Vincent de Paul: a Wesley, a Blumhardt, a William Booth, and an Albert Schweitzer, to cite a few names only. Everywhere the same uprooting—unintelligible, if there were not a faith in God, who gives life and retains the right to guide it.

"I believe in God." Alongside these dramatic personalities in whom the supernatural becomes manifest, innumerable hearts know God amid the obscurity of simple tasks, and strive to serve Him. The Calvinist rite places the chant of the psalms at the beginning of its Sunday worship. After the translation of Marot, those of Conrart and Piachaud nourish our piety.

Psalm 25 (24 in the Douay version) proclaims:

> To thee, O Lord, have I lifted up my soul.
>
> In Thee, O my God, I put my trust;

and Psalm 89:

> My God, it is you alone that I honor;
>
> I shall exalt you ceaselessly.
>
> My God, it is you alone that I adore;
>
> I shall bless you ceaselessly.

Like public prayer, personal prayer plays an essential role in the service of God. Protestantism, seen from without, may seem a half-lay religion, because of the sobriety and the rarity of its ceremonies. The appearance is deceitful. An excessive modesty generally restrains our people from speaking about themselves and of what they hold most in their hearts. In the intimacy of the family, in a hospital room, one confides in trust; and the role played by God in so many lives becomes clear. Those who take pen in hand are most verbose. In the writings of Pastor Charles Wagner, the author of *The Friend* and of *Youth*, his biographer has revealed this notation: "It is a really beautiful, a really great thing—Faith, deep certitude, and infinite serenity. It consoles us in our ignorances, our gropings, our faults, too . . . I ask only that for myself and for others. When I shall have seized this gleam, I shall make it beam over the world." (*Un Homme, Le Pasteur Charles Wagner,* by A. Wautier d'Aygalliers, Fischbacher, p. 97.)

In witness to this, the letters written by Suzanne Hoffmann de Visme during a serious illness, to her husband, who was pastor of the French Church in London and had to remain in his parish because of his duties while she was being taken care of in Switzerland, sound an echo close to ourselves. The last of these moving letters sum them all up: "Yes, my dear, I believe that God holds my life in His hands. Sometimes discouragements gripped me a little, when, after a pleasant recovery, I felt myself sink again. But God knows in Himself why, and that ought to be sufficient for us." (*Dieu sait pourquoi,* Labor, Geneva, p. 99.)

I could open the books of our theologians and show you texts from Karl Barth and Emile Brunner on the omnipotence of God. These plain citations seem preferable to me: they express profoundly the piety of our co-religionists. Under a familiar form, they keep alive the essential message of Luther, Zwingli, and Calvin. Is not such faith quite close to your own? You will say to me: "And your famous predestination! Does not that extraordinary doctrine raise a screen between the *Credo* of the Catholic and that of the Protestant?" On that particular point of theology, Calvin has scarcely any adherents among us. Predestination, which he had borrowed from St. Augustine, goes beyond the teaching of Scripture in the rigorous form which he gave to it. The immense majority of the Reformed today casts aside the idea that God chooses in advance some rare elect souls, and rejects forever the vast majority of men. The relations of free will and of grace are a mystery. Even Karl Barth, who, in reaction against the moralism of the declining nineteenth century, returns to the terminology of the sixteenth century, wants all men to be saved; we are in his eyes all lost and all redeemed: all Jacobs, all Esaus, all Peters, and all Judases. That is Origen more than Calvin.

From original Calvinism, there exists on this point only the cry: "Glory to God alone." To set God most high above everything, such is the desire of the best sons of the Reformation, and I do not doubt but that you yourself feel in perfect harmony with us on this point. The unity of Christians is discovered, and the word "fraternity" is fitting on the terrain of the *Credo*.

You may find me, my dear Canon, too optimistic, but if I look at those who have expunged God from their interests, I can only feel unaccountably close to the others who yet bend down before Him and who look, even now, with hope towards Him. God is an article of faith; God is not a truth which is self-evident. Many bypass it without seeing it or repel it with irritation. Toward 1850 in Europe unbelievers were rare; since then, free-thinking, under the triple form of positivism, Marxism and existentialism, has cruelly shaken the ancient certitude. Today wherever a community proclaims "I believe in God," it no longer performs a trite act.

Kindly accept, dear Canon, the assurance of my respectful sentiments in our Lord.

JEAN RILLIET

8.

Reverend and dear Pastor,
Well and good! This time we are on the heights! We breathe a purer air than that of historical, theological or ecclesiastical

quarrels. We have the joy of meeting with all adorers of our God. It is not in the least useless to rest on this sweet thought at a time, when, as you say, the denial of the idea of God has made such appalling progress among men!

"God is an article of faith," you say. Yes, our God—to you Protestants as well as to us Catholics. Why? Because, even while admitting, as we Catholics do, and as undoubtedly many among you also do, that reason can demonstrate the existence of God, our God is not solely the result of a syllogism or of many. I shall express that by saying that our God is not a God of paper, but a God of fire. He is not an "inferred" God, a God, who, according to Voltaire, is the God-watchmaker, whom one must acknowledge "since the watch goes." No! He is a God, loved, adored, prayed to, dwelling very near us, dwelling in us, a God who makes of our soul His temple. On the other hand, He is not the One God revealed by the universe, but the One God-in-Three-Persons, revealed by Jesus Christ, notably in these words: "Go, teach all nations, baptizing them in the name of the Father and of the Son and of the Holy Ghost."

I consider as very precious that observation which you make: that the God whom you love and invoke is no longer the God of Luther or Zwingli or Calvin—I mean, the God of absolute predestination, which doctrine I shall not admit is that of St. Augustine, at least not without an explanation. Such a God is neither yours nor ours, because He would no longer be the God-Love, of whom St. John speaks. Absolute predestination, which you declare to be foreign to Scripture, presents to us a God who loves only the elect and deliberately abandons the reprobate to their horrible destiny—eternal fire—without any fault of theirs, since free will does not exist according to Luther, Zwingli and Calvin.

Let us set aside these frightening aspects. You repudiate them just as we do. That is an immense step taken by Protestantism since what you call the Reformation and what we call the Protestant Revolution.

Let us fix our gaze on the idea of God which is common to us. It is from there that we must take our departure in order to descend little by little the chain of Christian truths, to mark out the fatal point where our separation begins.

Suffer, then, that I impart to you my personal reflections, all founded on Catholic theology, concerning the idea of the One God and the Three Persons.

You are not unaware that the Church obliges her clerics to consecrate a certain time of each day to mental prayer (Canon 125 of Canon Law).

For many years now I have attached myself each day to thinking about God—I can say it in all sincerity and humility —and lo! what comes back to me continually and delightfully in spirit is this: God is the eternal Being. As the eternal Being, He is of necessity the infinite Good; for, being and goodness coincide in all their entirety. Evil is but a lack, an absence, a break, a discord, a false note, a disobedience. It is not a being, it is not of being, but it is of non-being.

That is what the old axiom means: *"Ens et bonum convertuntur:* being and goodness are interchangeable."

Goodness in its turn—that is to say, Being—is intimately inclined to expand. Latin says that in terms difficult to translate: *"Bonum est sui diffusivum:* goodness is of itself diffusive." It is a property of goodness to expand, to communicate itself, to give itself. But that is what we call love!

As St. John has said, God is charity. God is love. That, then, responds to the essence of God. God is not love by accident, but by essence. Every religion starts from there. There is no true religion without that faith. A chilling God, a God according to the manner of Voltaire, a God who is not providence, a God who could not be love, could not ask our love; which amounts to saying that he could not be our God.

From thence comes that joy which we experience when we

find in Holy Scripture expressions which show us God under this aspect: the God of fire, the God of goodness and paternity, the God of pity; the God who speaks familiarly with His children, who spoke with Abraham, with Agar in the desert; the God who was accustomed to speak with the prophets; the God who inspired the prophet of fire, Elias; and, above all, the God who sent His Son, and of whom St. John said, for that very reason, that "He loved the world so much."

I believe that in starting from this God, in descending little by little the chain of truths, as I said above, we shall come to the point of division where Protestants and Catholics separated. Yet let us savor with joy the happiness of conversing about the God-Love in whom we converge completely.

Our old scholastic authors, whom I believe to have been unjustly attacked at the time of the religious quarrels of the sixteenth century, had many a time turned their loving attention to God-Love, like ourselves. It was with a pleasant surprise that I met, in a recent study on Hugh of St. Victor (*L'Idée Chrétienne de l'Amour* by G. Dumeige, S.J., Paris, 1952), the following profound explanation of the Holy Trinity.

God is love, says Hugh of St. Victor. That means that God is supreme in love as in omnipotence. But, in order that love may exercise itself, it needs an otherness. God engenders His Word, which is in Him a second Person, without ceasing to be the same essence as Himself, just as—if one dares to make a comparison, withal imperfect in human things—the philosophic system of a thinker, the novel of a novelist, the tragedy or the comedy of a playwright, the theme of a musician, and the speculation of a learned man have in some sort their proper life in the thought which produces them without ceasing to be that thought itself!

In God-Love the essential need of otherness is the generation of the Word, but of a co-eternal Word, co-extensive, consubstantial with the Father. Between the Father and the

Word, an infinite love expresses itself by the presence of a Third Person, the issue of that love itself, whom we call the Holy Spirit. He who truly loves desires that his love expand and be divided. The Father and the Son claim a Third Person in an identical desire, whom they cherish in common, and who will be a response to their love! In this fashion, the Three Divine Persons are constituted.

All that, you will say, is metaphysical. Yet all that is charged with fire, too. And from thence everything proceeds. From thence, and in that way, everything is explained. If God is the Creator, it cannot be except by love. If God sends His Son to us, this can be only to show us His love, to demand ours in return, to *buy* it in some fashion, and *at what a price!*

Ah! how one understands in the light of these few reflections the touching statement which inspired this line of Charles Péguy: "Man refunds little for what he has cost!"

How one will understand, also, a much more important thing—that Jesus Christ, our Jesus, of whom we must speak together, should have pronounced that saying which should devour our hearts incessantly: "I am come to cast fire upon the earth, and what do I desire except that it be lighted" (Luke 12:49).

How well one understands, on the other hand, or in the same sense, that he has summed up the Law and the Prophets in this single precept: "Thou shalt love the Lord thy God with thy whole heart, with thy whole mind, with thy whole strength, and thou shalt love thy neighbor as thyself!"

If God is love—as we believe, as all Scripture testifies, as the coming of Christ, His whole life, His whole teaching, as His death above all cries out to us, as reason itself proclaims— just as I said while speaking of the identity of being and goodness, then of goodness and love, we must establish ourselves on this path never to leave it. The foundations of Christ must spring forth from there; it is in His Sacred Heart, according to Catholic thinking, that everything has taken birth, and it is through that Sacred Heart that everything must be explained. In the same way I heard my venerated master of theology, Cardinal Billot, say it more than fifty years ago: "In piercing the side of Jesus with his lance, the unknown soldier, whom tradition calls Longinus, obeyed without knowing it, an order from on high; for nothing happens in religious ritual, as in the case of the sacrifice of the Cross, without the will of the supreme disposer. That was the *signature* on the drama itself: Love wished, Love marked it out, Love accomplished it!"

We are now engaged in the profundity of our Christianity. Let us then follow our route.

Kindly accept, dear Pastor, my very devoted and fraternal sentiments in our Lord.

L. CRISTIANI

V

† / †

"Creator of Heaven and Earth"

9.

Dear Canon Cristiani,

The authors of the ancient formula of baptism briefly end their affirmation of God and His existence by these words: "Creator of heaven and earth." God is no stranger to reality; everything that lives proceeds from Him and belongs to Him. The believer recognizes this dominion and strives to inscribe it effectively in his life and in the human society about him: "Thy kingdom come, thy will be done on earth as it is in heaven," each of us prays in his worship. Wherever the Our Father is recited in the light of the *Credo*, an incentive seizes those who are associated in this holy prayer, unless they pray mechanically. Truly meditated on, this text, so brief and so condensed, recalls the universal belonging of men to God. It urges us to take it seriously and points out the ways of true progress.

The Marxists repeat with great emphasis that they have discovered the social problem. It seems that, according to them, nobody before them has noted poverty. They would be astonished, if they should take pains to open our sermon books, to see to what degree liberal preachers have shaken off the lethargy of our faithful in the churches. For example, Adolphe Monod, an outstanding preacher of Paris, scolded his parishioners severely on the day after the Revolution of 1848: "I say," he cried with the freedom that becomes a minister of the Gospel, "one would not have attacked property, if it had been administered according to the views of God. The rich, alas! thought only of themselves. We saw them always selfish under different names, now avaricious, now generous to a fault, now burying their treasure in the earth, now casting it away in indulgence, in extravagances, in vanity, if not in lust and sin."

Some years later, Eugene Bersier, whose eloquence made the élite of Parisian Protestantism run to the Taitbout Chapel and then to the Church of the Star under the reign of Napoleon III and MacMahon, recalled the principal truths of a living Christianity: "Brethren, if you are Christians, there is a minimum to which all men have a right; namely, the right to be able to live while saving their souls. Indeed, I declare, after having weighed this word before God, who hears me, that there are conditions where that is impossible, short of a miracle. There is a degree of misery where one loses at last all sense of dignity; there is in our factories a promiscuity which kills shame and which soils the soul. There is in the crushing work of children, condemned to being nothing more than machinery, an absolute barrier to their moral development. There is in slavery the death of all Faith and of all religion."

Thus speak out the servants of the Word. The same preoccupation haunts laymen like Sismondi, the son of a pastor, an outstanding economist and literateur, who, at the end of the Empire, perceived the aberration of a fierce rivalry which sacrificed workers to the profits of business, and who published in 1819, before the time expected, his *Nouveaux Prin-*

cipes de l'Economie Politique, wherein the progress of a blind Liberalism is masterfully shown. The agitations which have overwhelmed Europe for forty years are the ransom money paid for its prolonged deafness. Why was it that true Christians were only a handful? Why this conspiracy of stifling which limited the range of their voices? The faithfulness of a few, however, saved the honor of the Church and prepared for the future. In each generation, the zealous fought against the lukewarm. It is of the first that it is said: "You are the salt of the earth."

If, however, the conviction that heaven and earth belong to God condemns a selfish stagnation, don't you think that it protects us against scepticism in social affairs today? Man in these days ends up in despair after the shocks he has undergone and after his noble dreams are consummated in blood. He is tempted to conclude with Sartre that "life glides along toward nothing" and to let the skiff of the city, like that of the family, founder. Moral effort is born of faith in God. That assures us that our existence here below has a meaning. If heaven awaits us, the earth is a stepping stone to it, and the believer has no right to disinterest himself in it. Because God created the earth, it is susceptible to justice.

Oh! I know, like you, the power of sin that transforms human relations into disorder. Yet the order of God condemns disorder; it engages us in a ceaseless fight against all sorts of deviation in us and about us. Protestantism, you know, repudiates asceticism under the monastic form, but it wages an analogous combat under a different form. Puritanism, in which all of us participate more or less, is also a protest against a dissolute life. The body and the soul are holy because God made them. We must protect them from all evil, a difficult undertaking and sometimes exhausting, in which we happen to stumble, but in which Christ the Saviour helps us conquer.

Furthermore, I would like to tell you something about the

family. I have one. I know the joys and the sorrows of it. Children, those gifts of God, often cause us much worry, but their presence about us enlarges our heart in a very singular way. I do not wish here to discuss ecclesiastical celibacy, a subject of division, but to underline what importance we attach to the purity and seriousness of the family, just as you do, because we see therein a divine institution. The eternal God said: "It is not good for man to be alone. I shall make for him an aid like unto himself" (Gen. 2:18). Later on He gives the command: "Increase and multiply." The family is the sanctuary where the body and the heart of the child is formed. Mother and father watch over him and communicate to him their experience of life and their faith. The wife accompanies her husband in all his preoccupations; her constant presence by his side is power for him. Physical desire cannot be separated from their spiritual vocation. Do you not agree with us in this battle for purity of morals?

Because of God the Creator, the corporal and the moral life of a being are sacred. Christianity opposes its constant appeals to the scorn which kills the humane in man. I am convinced that our Churches play the role of a witness of God for our people, as your Church does for those whose existence she directs. It often happens that I discuss their obligations with adolescents and young men. I am then bound by the feeling of being to them the echo of a voice infinitely more essential than my own. Those eager eyes, those lips desirous of tenderness, those hearts which hide under a simulated rudeness belong to God, their Creator. He made them for work and for love. They will fashion the tools which will nourish them; they will clasp in their arms the woman who will deliver their sons and daughters. Yet the effort and the delight are not the supreme end. The soul develops or dries up in them and through them. "What will it profit a man to gain the whole world and suffer the loss of his own soul?" warned our Lord. This mysterious reality of the soul fixes a boundary to impassioned transport as to legitimate ambition. It channels the human effort, all the time placing before man the hope of a fulfillment in eternity. All that, my dear Canon, would demand supplementation and a pen better qualified than mine. I have the assurance that on reading me, despite such a lack of detail, you will feel close to the Pastor who is writing to you, and who knows that he is united to you by faith in the one omnipotent God.

JEAN RILLIET

10.

Reverend and dear Pastor,
Before replying to today's letter, I would like to stress a little point concerning the doctrine of St. Augustine on predestination.

I seem to understand from your preceding letters that that doctrine is the same one which Luther—and, after him, Calvin—taught, and which has been, you tell me, practically abandoned by Protestants in our times. On this point I am not of your opinion. A major difference exists between the doctrine of St. Augustine and that of Luther and Calvin; to wit, that the former professes belief in free will aided by grace, while the latter do not admit any cooperation on our part with the work of salvation, which, according to them, is entirely, totally and exclusively the work of divine grace.

You are certainly aware that we are going to celebrate, next September, the sixteenth centenary of the birth of St. Augustine with a huge international congress to take place in

Paris from the twenty-first to the twenty-fourth. On that occasion a certain number of reports presented to the congress will be published. The work is actually in the press, and in this collection I have been allowed to contribute a study entitled *Luther and Saint Augustine*. In this report I prove three things: (1) that Luther, although an Augustinian religious, did not begin to study the works of the illustrious patron of his Order except by chance— "*casu*," as he himself says; (2) that he found an extreme joy therein, and that he believed that he had discovered a precious confirmation of his own ideas on predestination; (3) that he became aware of his error later on, but that he continued to refer to St. Augustine, all the while knowing that the great Doctor could not be used as a defender of justification by faith without good works. And I cite, pertinent to this, a letter written by Melancthon at the end of May 1531, from Wittemberg with the consent of Luther, who affixed his signature to it. The whole letter should be cited. But I shall choose the following passage: "Augustine does not fully express the view of Paul, although he is closer to it than the Scholastics. And I, I cite Augustine as wholly conformed to our doctrine . . . because of public persuasion, although he does not explain justice by faith in a satisfactory manner. . . ."

This authorization by Melancthon would be accused of lack of scientific probity by many critics. He continued to say, while he knew the opposite to be true, that Augustine taught the same doctrine as Luther and did so "because of public persuasion, *propter publicam de eo persuasionem*." I fear that this was not very honest! (See the letter in question in Endre, *Luthersbriefwechsel*, IX, 18–20).

By a natural transition, I come from that observation on your letter to the words: "Creator of heaven and earth."

Truly it is the existence of liberty which gives creation its total value and permits it to attain its end. What, then, is this end? It would not be to believe in God the Creator to the extent of admitting that He created without a purpose, to have a plaything, to distract Himself—if one dare to speak so, which one cannot do without blaspheming!

We have once again found our debate of the other day: liberty is not an end in itself, but only the condition for attaining it.

Liberty is not the end because it is essentially ambivalent (that is, mutually attracted to and repulsed from an object). It can turn toward good or evil, love or hatred.

Liberty is the faculty of choice. But there is the choice left to be made. I strongly believe that there can be no difference between us with respect to this. The descriptions which you make of your pastoral activities lead to this: to encourage good and to avoid evil. In a word, to clarify and to aid liberties in their choice.

What is the supreme end of creation? Evidently, it is the very aim of our life, which is *the possession of God through love!*

In creation, degrees of perfection exist. There are levels of different "kingdoms." This is the place to recall that familiar passage from Pascal:

"All bodies—the firmament, the stars, the earth and its kingdoms—are not equal to the least of intelligent spirits; for the latter knows all that and himself; bodies know nothing.

"All bodies together and all spirits together, and all their works, are not equal to the least movement of love. For that is of an infinitely higher order.

"From all bodies assembled, one could not succeed in making a single small thought; that is impossible and of another order—the supernatural."

Charles Péguy, of whom I am not making a prophet, but who has thought out his catechism cogently, says this in his turn: "There are five kingdoms: mineral, vegetative, animal, human and Christian: there is no less deviation, no less approach, no less discontinuance between the third and the fourth, and between the fourth and the fifth, than between any of the other three."

You and I think that all the inferior kingdoms were created only in view of the superior ones. "All is yours," said St. Paul.

In the final analysis, then, everything was created because of love, because of the law of charity, because of the "Christian kingdom." The human kingdom is encircled by the animal, vegetative and mineral kingdoms; and in its turn the Christian kingdom begins from the human kingdom.

But the final end, the end to attain, the one for which liberty (of which we have spoken at length) was given to man, is love.

When one reflects on this, one sees clearly that it cannot be otherwise. God is love, not by accident, by chance or contingency, but by His essence, by His most inward essence. Love explains everything in Him and in the Holy Trinity itself, although it remains a mystery to our weak intelligence. Being essential Love, God cannot create except through love, He cannot create except for love. By giving to a creature, be it angel or man, the power to love, He made it as like to Himself as possible. Love is essentially a choice. Without liberty, there is no love.

Once more we encounter the exalted divine precept: "You shall love the Lord your God with your whole heart, with your whole soul, with all your strength, and you shall love your neighbor as yourself."

Our Lord said expressly that this precept is not from Him, but that it was in the Law, buried, it is true, in an endless list of positive and negative commandments. He disengaged it, set it off with admirable mastery. We shall see, while speaking about our Lord in the ensuing exposition of our common *Credo*, how far He urged both; that is, how He loved God His Father, and men His brothers.

You justly touch upon, Reverend and dear Pastor, the deficiencies of that Christian love which have permitted social relations to become poisoned in such a regrettable manner. What I would reproach Marxism with is, not at all for reminding one of the obligation of social justice and social fraternity, but for having lowered the social problem to the material level of well-being on this earth; for having closed the horizon to the eyes of man, for denying God, the soul, eternity and the infinite; and finally for having based its actions on class hatred, which is the contrary of love.

Thus, it is impossible to arrive at any other result than what we see spreading out before our horrified eyes: incurable mistrust among peoples, secret armaments unceasingly more dreadful, fear—or, rather, lasting terror—of a war which would signal the end of a world, and possibly the end of this world.

Return to the Gospel is the only possible remedy for so many evils which threaten us all, and especially the younger generations, of whom you speak as the father of a family, conscious of your divine responsibilities.

While discussing these matters, you touch on a fiery problem: ecclesiastical celibacy, on one hand, and what you call monastic asceticism, on the other.

I shall reply briefly to these two points.

Ecclesiastical celibacy has its source in the sentiment of a spiritual fatherhood, superior to a physical fatherhood, as sublime and legitimate as that may be. The ecclesiastic has his origin in the example and words of celibate Christ, in the example and words of the apostle St. Paul. I shall not insist on this for the moment. We shall return to it, should you judge it necessary.

As to monastic asceticism, I would ask your permission to cite a personal experience. I was presiding, some days ago, over an investiture of the habit in a congregation of religious whose occupation is linked with the apostolate of the press, consisting in bringing the Bible, and especially the Gospel, from house to house, as well as the lives of Jesus and the saints who give the most eloquent commentary on Holy Scripture. Two young girls about twenty years old were enrolling in this admirable ministry. In the presence of a large congregation who desired to witness the ceremony, I had only to cite and summarize the recent encyclical of Pope Pius XII on Sacred Virginity. The Pope proves in it, without the shadow of a doubt, that marriage is a divine institution which Jesus made one of the sacraments of His Church; but that virginity—not any sort of virginity, but virginity offered, devoted and consecrated to God—had been put on a higher plane by the apostle St. Paul.

Then I cited and commented on this refrain from an ancient hymn taken from *The Banquet of the Ten Virgins* by St. Methodius of Olympus, who wrote about the year 300: "I keep myself pure for Thee, and with the lighted lamp in my hand I march, O my Spouse, to meet Thee!"

What is more beautiful than that young people consecrate themselves freely and enthusiastically to the service of God and of a humanity reborn in Jesus Christ?

Kindly accept, Reverend and dear Pastor, my very faithful affection in our Lord.

L. CRISTIANI

VI

† / †

"I Believe in Jesus Christ"

11.

Dear Canon Cristiani,

Protestant Churches, at least those belonging to the Reformed Rite, rarely contain a crucifix. I, for one, regret this and would willingly follow the example of the Lutherans and the Anglicans in whose churches a grieving Christ dominates the altar. However, in several of our churches, for a quarter of a century, large and simple wooden crosses have adorned a wall, clearly visible behind the communion table. The dislike for the crucifix is an inheritance of confessional struggles. Finding in it the symbol of those who were persecuting them, the Huguenots decided to be satisfied with the symbol of a Bible placed on a pulpit only. Is not the Bible the word of God and Christ the Word-made-flesh? This excess of austerity could be deplored: the historical reason which I have recalled explains it, even if it does not fully justify it.

But if the image of Christ is often absent from our sanctuaries, His Gospel, His Person, are nonetheless the center of our piety. "I believe in Jesus Christ, His only Son, our

Lord," proclaims the *Credo*. As a young child, the Protestant listens with wonder to the beautiful stories of Jesus. His mother recounts them to him with the help of an illustrated book. Having reached his sixth year, he joins Sunday school, where women monitors, ordinary lay people, benevolent helpers of the pastor, mingle prayer and the singing of hymns with the narrative of the miracles and the parables. Have you ever had the opportunity to visit a parish hall or a church, where, in each corner, ten to twelve wide-eyed children form a circle around the monitor? Or, after the prayer, have you heard their childish voices rise towards the Saviour of whom they have just been told? The music used in these hymns is, obviously, not worth much, and most of the organists consider it scornfully, but, thanks to it, the touching words sung with conviction are engraved forever on the hearts of the little ones:

> Merciful Saviour, faithful shepherd,
> Lead us by your love,
> And with your fatherly hand
> Nourish us from day to day.
> Blessed are you, merciful Master;
> Jesus, we belong to you;
> To you alone we wish to belong;
> Blessed are you, our King.

The birth of Christ through Mary, His ministry of mercy, the hatred of the Pharisees, the abandonment by His disciples, the denial by Peter, the crucifixion, the placing in the tomb, and then the Resurrection are engraved little by little on their hearts and, with these, Faith enters for life. The catechism which we teach them when they are sixteen probably does not penetrate as deeply (but for a few exceptional cases) as this rudimentary training. From then on, should a crisis of conscience occur, the adolescent at war with his passions will return to the Name which he was taught to place above all other names so long ago; he opens the Gospel and reads it with a fervent desire to find truth! He finds it by find-ing Him who said, "I am the Truth."

Truth, for us, is identified with Christ Himself. That sweet Master, scourged by the Roman soldiers and condemned by Pilate, incarnates all the love and holiness of God. "God was in him reconciling men to himself," wrote St. Paul. God is identified with Him: that is the mystery which the dogma of the Trinity seeks to express. But we hardly even speak to our students of the Trinity; it is beyond them; it includes the unity of the Three Divine Persons under too dogmatic a form, too abstract for the children of this century. The cruci-fied Christ, on the other hand, expresses an eloquence to which the most uncultured, as well as the most cultured spirit, remains sensitive. "It is not to Christianity, it is to Jesus Christ that we must go," is the paradoxical advice of Alex-ander Vinet, the Vaudois thinker already quoted above, whose work has had such an influence among us.

I was present, the other day, at the farewells in his parish of a pastor whose age and sickness forced his retirement. He preached on the text of St. Paul: "I have wished to know among you one thing, Jesus Christ and Jesus Christ crucified." The assembled congregation showed deep deference by its attentive homage to the efforts made through divine worship, prayers, spiritual exchange, and catechism for many years to transmit the very voice of the Saviour into their hearts. I think that this sermon theme could be chosen by the majority of my colleagues.

Jesus Christ is the Saviour of the world! We have said this so much and repeated it so often that the fear of weakening and wearing it away is born. But contact with souls teaches that wherever the certitude "He has died for me" penetrates, wherever the gaze is fixed on the Cross, a revolution takes place, pride is extinguished and pain overcome. That is why the Ecumenical Assembly which will take place in the coming days at Evanston has chosen for the theme of its works the statement "Jesus Christ, only hope of the world."

In childhood, the presence of Christ here below is accepted without demur. Later on, one is astonished to see this perfect life inscribed in the midst of our unhappy life: "He was conceived of the Holy Spirit." God is the source of this foolish enterprise, which consists in delivering Himself to men without defense and in dying in their midst and at their hands in order to deliver them from sin! "And He is born of the Virgin Mary." Mary is the pliant instrument of grace. We do not say of her more than does the *Credo*, but what it says we believe. Calvin, commenting on the *Magnificat*, points out in Mary the model of the believer: "Mary," he states, "is blessed insofar as she believed." Having accepted with faith the angelic greeting, she "conceived and brought forth her salvation and that of the whole world." If Mary had refused the task which God in His sovereign wisdom had destined for her, the world would have perished in darkness. Each one, in imitation of her, must go where God sends him, speak where He asks him to speak, serve where his service is needed. It will be the eternal glory of Mary, the Mother of Christ, that she has bound up her person in that of her Son. Thus she opens up the list of those women whose faith the Gospel describes and whose memory, because of it, will never perish. To her, in the first place, is applied the text pronounced in regard to the sister of Lazarus: "In truth, I say to you, wherever this gospel will be preached in the whole world, what she has done will also be recounted in memory of her" (Mark 14:4).

I have the habit in catechism class of linking closely the remembrance of what our Lord did for us to the lessons on the two sacraments of baptism and the Lord's Supper. Jesus Christ, His message, His life offered in ransom for our faults, and His Resurrection are the purifying waters announced by the prophet Ezechiel, as well as the nourishing bread and the thirst-quenching wine necessary for the regeneration and the growth of the soul. A little water poured on the head of a child: this is materially nothing, and yet, behind the symbolic act, stretches the long series of stages during which the liberating dialogue, started on this very morning, will continue. Jesus Christ will address Himself to the soul of the selfish child, which we all are; He will pardon him and free him, little by little, from his idolatrous attachments and from the fear which echoes in him, a man of the twentieth century, the distant fear of Adam. Jesus Christ will attach him to God, from whom he is separated. In the face of Him who is the Light of the world, the darkness in him will be dispelled. The "visible sign of an invisible grace," to take up the celebrated formula of St. Augustine, baptism is a prelude to the mystery of Faith, which links the soul to its Saviour. For us it is not baptism that saves, but the grace visibly represented by baptism; that is, speaking in a very rudimentary manner, the action of Christ, who pardons and who transforms. In saying "I believe in Jesus Christ," I see again the crowd of small babies for whom I have been, through the sacrament, like a simple instrument—and I wish to make this clear—simply their doorman into Christian life, some of them kicking in a small play suit, others sleeping peacefully in their long dresses of white muslin. I was, at that moment, the representative of Him who snatches them from nothingness, if at least they open their ears and their eyes to receive Him. "Behold, I stand at the door and knock, if any one hear my voice I shall enter in and I shall sup with him and he with me," warns the Apocalypse in its mystical language.

The Lord's Supper is also the avowal of Jesus Christ. Whoever advances towards the holy table asks for Him and receives Him. To the gesture and the visible gifts correspond in the secret of the heart an imploring and a granting; a real Presence, which is not localized for us in the Sacrament but of which He is both the promise and the occasion. We receive our communicants, you know, behind a simple wooden table covered with a white tablecloth on which are placed a plate and a silver cup containing the bread and the wine. The officiating pastor gives out to the faithful one after another a fragment of this bread, which recalls that Jesus Christ died for them; while a counsellor of the parish, representing the lay element of the community, hands them the cup. The words of institution have been recited beforehand: "This is my body which is broken for you; this is my blood which is shed for many for the remission of sins." These serious and strained faces which file before me, one after another, these hands taking from my hand the small white square which recalls the Saviour dead for them—I know nothing more touching. The ceremony would be incomprehensible, absurd, without faith. They came because they believed, repeating within themselves the words of St. Peter: "Lord to whom shall we go but to thee? Thou hast the words of eternal life and we have believed and we have known that thou art the Holy one of God" (John 6:68–69). The Communion is man, with all his humanity, uniting himself to God, in all His divinity: not that the difference between the creature and the Creator disappears; the child refinds his Father, that is all; but that is immense; and Christ, the Son of God, is the instrument of that reconciliation. If He had not accepted our condition, a poor livery under which He conceals His divinity, the meeting would not take place. "God is Love," you recalled in your first letter on the *Credo*. The Lord's Last Supper, each time that it is celebrated, depicts before our eyes that essential truth. No one, more than the officiating minister, measures the abyss which separates him from God. He has the habit of self-analysis: all the vanities assail his imperfect heart each day; Jesus Christ by the blood He shed expiates the past and, firm bastion against satanic powers, guarantees the future.

If we seek what unites Christians, whatever be the denomination to which they belong, is it not in their Communion with Christ that we discover it? What I have tried to explain here, do you not also feel face to face with the Saviour, even if our rites are different? On reading your reflections on God and on the Trinity, I measured the short distance between what you believe and what we believe. God is Love. The miracle of Christ is to make that love accessible to us, and—having made it incarnate in His brief life, which extended from the census of Caesar Augustus to the moment when Pontius Pilate governed Judea—to permit all men from age to age to know God such as He is in His eternal and inexhaustible love!

Kindly accept, my dear Canon, the assurance of my devoted sentiments in our Lord.

JEAN RILLIET

12.

Reverend and dear Pastor,
Discussing Jesus Christ, His Gospel and the truth which He has brought into the world is for me, just as it would be for any Catholic, a profound joy! It is here, thank God, that we again find a large field of common interest. I will tell you, in a moment, my full thought on this subject. But I am happy to note that you are of the number of Protestants who regret this excessive austerity which the fratricidal quarrels of the sixteenth century have left in your Churches. You admit that the "cult of images," so ancient in the Church, so natural, so conformable to human nature and so well adapted in particular to the tendency of children and to all those who, by their simplicity and innocence either retained

or refound, resemble them, as Jesus Christ wished, not only
is not so condemnable as the disciples of Calvin believe it
to be (according to Calvin's doctrine) but that it could be of
great use in sustaining or awakening piety among Christians.
It is not in an age like ours, when more and more use is made
of images in teaching, that one should forbid images in religious instruction and education.

That said, I liked very much these lines in your letter of
today: "But if the image of Christ is often absent from our
sanctuaries, His Gospel, His person are not less at the center
of our piety."

On this, we are in complete agreement. And I cannot
resist the pleasure of prolonging your thought on what is in
complete agreement with Catholic thought.

What is Jesus Christ for a Catholic?

Jesus Christ is the Son of God made Man. He is "Em-
manuel" or "God with Us" predicted by the great Isaias. He
is the Word of God, who was in the beginning—that is to
say, before the beginning of all creation—at the side of God,
in God, and who was God. He is the same Word who "was
made flesh and dwelt among us."

He is, at the same time, perfect God and perfect Man. He
is a single divine Person with two natures, the divine and
the human. He is also, according to the word of Saint Paul,
the new Adam, the second Adam, who repaired the evil
caused to the whole of Adam's posterity by original sin, by
returning us to the life of grace, from which sin had snatched
us.

It is He who defines Himself by saying: "I am the Good
Shepherd and I know my sheep and my sheep know me. . . .
I give my life for my sheep. . . ."

He is, in brief, and always in the very terms which He has
chosen, the One who declared: "I am the Way, the Truth
and the Life!"

He is the Way because no one can go to His Father without

passing through Him. He is the Truth because all His teaching is sacred, divine, intangible, absolute and, because, outside of this teaching, there is no truth capable of leading us to eternal salvation. Finally, He is the Life because outside of Him there has been given to man, in this world or in the other, no other way of living in God, who is the Source of life and holiness. That is what St. Peter, in one of his first discourses, as narrated in the Acts of the Apostles (4:12), proclaimed forcefully: "There is salvation in no other, for no other name has been given under Heaven to man by which we must be saved."

All that you admit as we do. All that you preach as we do. It is in that that we are Christians, both of us. I will go further still; it is by that that we are "Catholics," all of us, you as well as myself. I mentioned a few minutes ago, that I intended to develop my whole way of thinking on the subject of our agreement, at least partially on what concerns Jesus Christ, the center of our faith and our piety. Very well! My thought is this: whoever believes in Jesus Christ, adores Jesus Christ, obeys Jesus Christ and wants to submit himself in everything to the will of Jesus Christ, *is implicitly and intentionally Catholic,* even if, as a consequence of his formation and as a result of the preconceived ideas he has inherited from his environment, he finds himself, in point of fact, outside the Catholic Church. You have, I know, Reverend dear Pastor, too realistic an esteem of the Roman Catholic Church to be offended by what I have just said. But you certainly know that we distinguish between belonging to the body of the Church and belonging to its soul. We count, certainly not in our statistics, but in our thoughts and in our affection, all baptized persons as belonging to the Catholic Church. Why is that? Because there is only one baptism, because this baptism is desired by Jesus Christ, because His Church—which, according to us (and we shall have to come back to this point), is the Catholic Church—has received the deposit of this baptism as of all revealed truth; and consequently she looks upon all those who have received baptism, administered simply in order to "do whatever Jesus Christ wished and commanded," as her own.

Starting from what moment do children, baptized in the dissident Churches—Protestant or Greek Schismatic—cease, according to us, to be Catholic? Starting only from the moment when they make an act of formal and personal adhesion to a Church which is not in communion with Rome.

But even at that moment, they continue to belong to the soul of the Catholic Church, if they are in good faith—that is, in what we call "invincible good faith": a sincere and straightforward good faith which has not the material or the moral possibility of instructing itself more completely.

To do what Jesus Christ wants, to follow Jesus Christ wherever He leads us, not to draw back before any sacrifice in order to obey His instructions, to respond to His infinite love for us—that, then, is to be *Catholics by intention.*

It will, therefore, be to the task of discovering the means each of our two Churches proposes to obey Jesus Christ in everything, that the letters which we are to exchange ought to be devoted.

While waiting, let us cast a glance together over the road which we have already travelled.

We have raised ourselves, first of all, up to God. We have contemplated Him in the Unity of His substance and the Trinity of His Persons. But we have lingered with pleasure on the thought that "God is Love."

By that love, we have explained the fact of creation and what is much more important: that, in this creation, there is a meaning—what we often call "the meaning of history"—and that this meaning was to result in intelligent and free beings capable of love. These beings are ourselves! All our grandeur is there. All our beauty is in this. We were created to the image and likeness of God, because we alone in the visible creation are capable of knowing and loving.

Today, in speaking of Christ, we have reached the central part of our Faith, that in which love of God reaches its zenith, above which it could never rise—the Incarnation of the Word; and that in which the love of man for God has reached its supreme limit: the sacrifice of Christ on the Cross. The line has not been broken for one single instant. Starting from love, we have remained in love, and we end with that supreme love of Christ for His Father, on one hand, and for us, on the other. Now we can understand those sublime words of Christ: "I have come to bring fire upon the earth and I desire nothing but that that fire be kindled! . . . Remain in my love! . . . If anyone love me, my Father will love him also and we shall come and dwell within him."

Therein is contained a whole program of love, a whole life. It is in this that Jesus is the Way, the Truth and the Life.

Up to this point, I believe, we agree completely. But, although it irks me to denounce here the imperfection, the insufficiency and the limited aspect of this agreement, I would be going against our promise if I stopped there. It is understood that we are talking freely, frankly, courteously, but nonetheless, firmly, each according to his own beliefs.

I shall, therefore, try to mention the points on which I differ from you.

There happens here what happens more than once when we Catholics hear a Protestant allocution over the radio. How many times have I not been questioned by Catholic listeners on this subject, especially when it was the voice, warm and grave, virile and eloquent, of the Pastor Marc Boegner that came over the air waves. "But," I would be told, "all that seemes as though it were preached by a Catholic preacher!"

In the same manner, if I were to read to Catholics what you say in your letter about the love of Jesus Christ, or those touching farewells of one of your pastor friends who commented on this text of St. Paul's: "I have wanted to know amongst you only Jesus Christ and Jesus Christ crucified," there is no doubt that they would exclaim: "But that is exactly what you preach yourself!"

I would then be compelled to show them that our language is not completely identical and even that there are serious differences between Protestants and Catholics.

Your manner of speaking of Mary, the Mother of the Saviour, is respectful, we admit, but cold. It does not render all the power of that title: "Mother of God." It is part of a general doctrine, by virtue of which Calvinism rejects the cult of the saints.

This is the first point of disagreement which will deserve, perhaps, an explanation between us later on.

Then, talking of the sacraments, you speak of two and only two, while we admit and practice seven. Another point of disagreement.

Of the sacraments which you admit, we are almost in complete agreement—and I have mentioned this before—as regards baptism, so that all the little ones who are baptized are, in our sight, real Catholics. But we meet a serious difference, a very serious one, as regards the "Lord's Supper." It is, for you, no more than the "symbolical avowal of Jesus Christ." And you add: "There corresponds to the visible acts and gifts, *in the secret of the heart,* an imploring and a fulfillment, *a real Presence, which is not localized for us in the Sacrament,* but of which this is at once the promise and the occasion."

Yet that is very far from responding to the Catholic Faith, which admits and teaches *a real Presence in the Sacrament itself, in virtue of transubstantiation.*

One God on the altar, one God in the sacred Host—that is undoubtedly tremendous! Yet we find here one of our most sensitive and most regrettable differences. I know well that we are no longer in the detestable period of the Affair of the "Placards," when the Holy Mass was denounced by Protestant posters as an abomination, and when Calvin himself never spoke of the sacred Host without designating it by the contemptuous expression "their Wafer"!

That there has arisen between us such differences in official teaching—I do not speak of disputable opinions, doubtful ones and consequently free ones, but of doctrines essential to salvation—it is there that the drama, the sorrowful drama, the great tragedy of the history of Christianity is found in modern times.

Yet, at this point, perhaps, it will be easier for us to detect the very origin of these differences. We have already spoken of the Church. I told you, then, that we could not settle the debate at once, that we must in the beginning ascend the ladder of the great revealed truths; first of all, to God, then to pass from there to Creation, to original sin, and to the Incarnation of the Word.

Here is how the question presents itself in all its restrictive force: Jesus Christ, for you as well as for us, is the Way, the Truth and the Life. But what has He done to be this, even to the end of the world? What has He done to assure the future of His mission? What has He done for the safekeeping of the deposit of salvific truth throughout the whole long span of the centuries? That He had done nothing at all would seem unlikely, I dare say, even discouraging; let us go further, it would be for men, for those hungry and thirsty for salvation and for truth, as we are, the most terrible of scandals.

It is here that one finds our most deplorable difference, which is the basis for all the others; for *we* say: "Jesus Christ has provided for the maintenance of His truth in the world forever by *a hierarchic Church, visible, indefectible and infallible.*"

If I understand your teaching clearly, your reply would be: "No, not by an infallible Church, incarnated in a visible and responsible authority, but in an invisible Church, bearing an inspired and infallible book, the Bible." However, on this point I must let you speak; it is not for me to present your Protestant Faith. We can do nothing better than to redouble our sincerity and our frankness in the examination of this stupendous problem: the Bible or the Church? We say, "the two of them." It seems to me that you say: "The Bible alone." But what did Jesus Christ say?

It is in Him, my dear Pastor, that I beg you to accept my respectful and cordial feelings.

L. CRISTIANI

VII

† / †

The Hereafter

13.

Dear Canon Cristiani,

With the affirmation of the death, the burial, the descent into hell and the Resurrection, the Apostles' Creed directs our attention to the extent of the reconciliation effected by Christ. Nothing escapes His mercy. He was not content to live and to teach. He, the Lamb delivered up for our sins, reaches the depths of our misery. He sinks with us into the darkness. His eyes are closed to the light. Willingly He immolates Himself and joins us in our fragility and in our mortality. I understand the effort of the ancient Doctors distinguishing in Jesus, in the presence of this abasement, the man who died and the God who could not die. However, despite this justifiable division, somewhat overdone, the mystery remains intact: Why a God-Man? St. Anselm questions: "Why did God become man?" We can add: "How could God be a man in the full sense of the word, even to the last pallor, even to the final death rattle, when the features contracted in pain finally grow limp on a cross?" Jesus died, as all of us shall die one day; just as we have so often seen death.

It is the sad but wonderful obligation of the pastor as of the priest to visit the sick, to assist the dying, to console those who are in mourning. Where the atheist sees only a ridiculous ending, we promise the return to life—and this at the precise time when death is being installed as the victor. In all my ministry, the most touching remembrance is probably that of the instant when I uttered in a loud voice Christ's words to an old woman, hunched in her bed and already half-destroyed by disease, who could no longer see nor speak: "I am the Good Shepherd, I am the Way, I am the Truth, I am the Resurrection and the Life." I suddenly saw her lips move and, after a third and hopeless effort at communication; I finally heard the word which reached me with difficulty as I was bent over the poor figure, a "Thank you," hardly distinct, an interpretation of the joy diffused by the promises of Jesus Christ in a soul still present in the body.

Sorrow here below is, at moments, already a sample of hell, but the *Credo* affirms that Christ descended into the abode of the dead. This part of the text concerns, in the first place, the souls who slept before the coming of the Son of God, as Peter (I, 3:19) and, after him, Justin Martyr, Clement of Alexandria and St. Irenaeus taught. Perhaps this text also envisages, by anticipation, all those possessed by Satan, those of yesterday and those of today? If His mercy could once cross the uncrossable threshold, must we not conclude that the most terrible and the most merited punishment does not stop His mercy? Must we distinguish in reality between purgatory and hell? I only point out here some perspectives and questions over which the theologians of the different confessions will certainly not reply in the same way. Our ancient Reformed dogmaticians knew only paradise and hell. The nineteenth century proposed a limited suffering for some, and a total destruction for the impenitent. The twentieth century, with Karl Barth, readmits the universal restoration of Origen. The limits imposed on a letter do not permit me to develop here my personal viewpoint of the problem. Let me define simply the fear which the two extreme theses inspire in me in the face of the *Credo*: the eternity of hell, and a universal and almost automatic restoration. A day will come, according to St. Paul, when God will be all in all (I. Cor. 15:28); which supposes, it seems to me, either the conversion of the rebels or their annihilation.

For the penitent and believing soul these problems do not present themselves. "Today you will be with me in paradise," said Jesus Christ to the converted robber who died at His side. The pardon is not distinct from the Resurrection: by His Ascension, the Saviour opens to us the gates of heaven. He who suffered and who was buried is refound on high and greets us. Face to face with death I dare, then, say, "True life begins." Christianity alone, in all its forms and in all its sanctuaries, authorizes such audacity to its messengers. At the end of *Being and Nothingness,* Sartre cites a parable of Kafka: "A merchant comes to plead at the castle; a horrible guard bars the entrance. The merchant dares not disregard him, waits, and dies while waiting. At the hour of death, he asks the guard: 'How does it happen that I was the only one to wait?' The guard replies: 'This gate was made for you alone.'" To the gate constructed but barred to him who would never go through it, the Gospel replies by the vision of Christ the Conqueror. To Existentialism—which is satisfied with affirming: "Each person realizes only one situation, his own," and which compares us to the slave who revolts in his chains and dies in the course of his thwarted attempt—we counter with the glorious memory of the Ascension. "Sits at the right hand of the Father," the *Credo* states; that is to say, right next to the Creator in the splendor of His Love.

"From whence He will come to judge the living and the dead:" the resurrected Christ will be my judge and the judge of all men. I find in this recollection a tremendous consolation, for the Christ who judges is the same as the Christ who has mercy. Through Him, because of Him, I can hope in every mercy and in all attenuation. The trial will not be pleaded before a pitiless judge. Is it not a text of St. John which, curiously enough, combines the judge and the lawyer: "If anyone has sinned, we have an advocate beside the Father, Jesus Christ the Just One" (I John 2:1)? The Father represents here the justice of God; and the Son, His mercy. Justice will never be deprived of love, nor love of justice. A justice without love would be terrible, a love without justice would be weakness.

Jesus Christ will come back and judge. In face of that certitude human powers grow weak. He who was supremely humbled will be also supremely exalted: empires, republics, democracies and churches will be weighed. It is neither you nor I who will decide the eternal fate of our fellow beings. You know how often our insight is found to be at fault: we judge on appearances; we let ourselves be limited; our criteria fail through an unconscious partiality. Above all, being sinners ourselves and saved by grace, we have no right to dispose of the fate of others. Jesus Christ, on the other hand, is explicit: "Judge not," says he, "in order not to be judged, for One will judge you as you have judged, and One will mete out to you with the measure with which you have meted out" (Matt. 7:1–2).

The judgment of Jesus Christ, capable of making the hypocrite and the slothful tremble, reassures the conscientious and faithful Christian. In the history of the ancient martyrs—at the time when the persecution of Septimus Severus waxed strong at Carthage—you recall the defiant apostrophe uttered by the victims against the proconsul who condemned them: "You judge us, but God will judge you in your turn." This cry often rose in the course of the centuries, and today—from the lips of those who are beaten down and badly treated for justice's sake—it still rises towards God. Here, in these conversations which we want to be perfectly sincere, we must say that, in the bosom of Christianity wherever a Christian has shed the blood of another Christian, whatever be his titles and his pretensions, it is on high that justice will be rendered. Violence in the bosom of the Church has caused a terrible evil in the course of the ages. You recall what we think of the burning at Servet. The Inquisition, St. Bartholomew's, the Revocation of the edict of Nantes and the Dragonnades, which precede and follow it, fall under the same condemnation, in our eyes at least.

In the last years of his life, Calvin carried on an epistolary discussion with the daughter of Louis XII, Renée of France, Duchess of Ferrari, a decided Huguenot, on a subject which was rather extraordinary and rather close to the one that holds our attention: Could the Duke of Guise, the son-in-law of the princess who had massacred hundreds of Protestants at Vassy and who had just died in his turn a violent death, be saved? The Duchess of Ferrari defends the memory of her son-in-law against certain fanatical pastors who consign him to hell. Calvin's reply is admirable. He explains his judgment on the evil done by the Duke: "Those who take up the sword will perish by the sword," as our Lord said. Calvin thinks that "Monsieur de Guise, who set the fire, could not be spared" although, in that which concerns himself, the Reformer had always discouraged vengeance. But, as regards eternal salvation, that is another question: "To damn him," he specifies, "is to go too far . . . for there is only one judge before the Judgment Seat to whom all of us render an account" (*Opera Calvini*, Vol. 20, Col. 246). And to discourage hasty judgments, as well as hatred, Calvin adds: "So, hatred and Christianity are incompatible. I mean hatred against persons. And it is contrary to the love which we owe them, [which is] to wish and even to procure their good, and exert ourselves insofar as we can to nourish peace and harmony with all" (*Op. cit.*, Col. 248).

Are not these reflections, preceding Servet's death by ten years, deserving to be made known? Such an exchange explains strikingly what the justice of Jesus Christ meant for two Protestants. The good Princess hopes for her son-in-law, although, she states, "I have never consigned him to a place wherever it may be," and says that she was not "so absorbed in him nor in my own children. . . . I know that he persecuted," she continues, "but I do not know nor do I believe, to tell you freely, that he was damned by God, for he gave signs to the contrary before dying" (*Op. cit.*, Col. 270 and 272).

Is it not to this sort of generous objectivity that we ought to tend? To place the justice of Jesus Christ above one's self obliges us to restraint. This episode drawn from religious wars will certainly interest the historian that you are. If history contains horrible pages, it includes rather beautiful ones.

Kindly accept, dear Canon, the expression of my fraternal regard in our Lord.

JEAN RILLIET

14.

Reverend and dear Pastor,

Your letter of today treats of the final destinies of man. It is here that our divine religion finds its full reason for existence. According to the words of Saint Paul, "If it is only for this life that we have put our hope in Christ, we are more worthy of pity than all other men" (I Cor. 15:19). It is not for this world that we are working, we priests of Jesus Christ, and you pastors of souls in the bosom of the Protestant Churches. We have the certitude of proceeding according to the interpretation of history, for this interpretation of history is the construction, day after day, of the heavenly Jerusalem. The Marxists pretend that "this interpretation of history" tends toward the establishment of a terrestrial city which would be the city of happiness for all. We are in agreement with them in desiring, as much as they, and perhaps more than they, the creation of a city of perfect social justice. I say "more than they," because that city is our desire through love and theirs through class-hatred. Even if that city should finally exist, it would not be for us Christians a final end. We believe in the celestial city, we believe in heaven, we believe in the immortality of the soul; and it is for this reason that death is not, in our eyes, a terminus but a beginning. It is for this that one of the most imperious obligations—and, as you say, most sorrowful—but also the most wonderful of a Christian pastor is to assist the dying in this passage from corporeal death to eternal life.

"To die is not to die, my friends, it is to change."

This line, from Lamartine's *The Death of Socrates,* finds an echo in another line of the great mystic John of the Cross:

"When you kill, it is to change death into life!"

Will you allow me to note the differences which exist between the spiritual succour given to the sick in your Churches and in ours? Faithful to your principle of salvation through Faith-confidence in Jesus Christ, you recall that Faith to the mind of the dying; you make him profess his belief in it even to the end. We can only approve the zeal which you exercise in this holy ministry.

First of all, we have the same approach; for without that, without Faith, confidence and charity, nothing can help the soul. As our theologians say, sacraments do not have their proper efficacy *ex opere operato* (from their administration) unless the conditions enumerated above precede. The sacraments do not act, as I have many times heard it said to me by way of objection and criticism, in a magical way, but they are instruments of grace; they are acts of Jesus Christ in person, sanctifying the souls which lend themselves freely and lovingly to them.

Yet a few of these sacraments are, according to us, of extreme efficacy at the moment of death. First of all, there is Confession. What a relief for the burdened conscience to be able to lay down its load of sins! Secondly, there is the Holy Eucharist, under the form of Viaticum, a divine provision for the journey. Nothing is more moving than the Communion of the dying! It is the prelude to the celestial Communion. It is the most wonderful preparation for it. Then it is sweet to recall the words of Christ: "Whoever eats my flesh and drinks my blood has life everlasting and I shall raise him up on the last day. . . . Whoever eats my flesh and drinks my blood, remains in me and I in him." (St. John 6:54-56).

Finally, we confer upon the dying the sacrament of the sick, which we call Extreme Unction, according to the saying of St. James: "Whoever among you is sick, let him have the priests of the Church come and let them pray for him, in anointing with oil in the name of the Lord; and the prayer of faith will save the sick man, and the Lord will restore him; and if anyone has committed sin, it will be pardoned him." (James 5:14-15).

It is impossible, according to us, that this prescription be an invention of St. James. Surely, he is treating of a sacramental institution coming from Jesus Christ.

From the care of the dying, we pass naturally into what we call "the hereafter."

Once more—and I beg you to excuse me—I appeal to something personal. One speaks, indeed, only of what one knows and of what one does!

The great firm Marietti, of Turin and Rome, is preparing

at this moment an outstanding work in Italian which will have for its title *The Mystery of the Hereafter in the Light of Revelation.* I have, before my eyes, the table of contents of the future volume. It suffices to read the titles of the chapters to know the essential points of Catholic doctrine on the hereafter: death, particular judgment, hell, limbo, purgatory, paradise. Naturally, one will treat in the preface the following themes: God is the final end of man, the soul is immortal, the destiny of the soul is submitted to an eternal predestination, but this predestination takes into account the prevision of the merits of man and of choices accomplished during his life by means of his free will.

There will be, too, chapters on the return of Jesus Christ at the end of the world, the resurrection of the body, universal judgment, and cosmic renovation.

But there will also be, and it is that which I wish to come to, a part entitled "Deviations and Errors." The publishers asked me, in this section, to write about the "deviations" of Protestantism in the sixteenth century. I did not have to speak of contemporaneous deviations. Your letter indicates very well that there are among you on this point—and particularly on the eternity of punishments and on the universal re-establishment—hesitations, waverings, different opinions. It is evidently on any one of these points where the need of the authority of a Church makes itself clearly felt—a Church gifted, in matters of faith and morals, with infallibility and therefore capable of settling by indisputable decisions controversies among Christians.

While treating of the Protestantism of the sixteenth century, I put the emphasis on the *rejection of purgatory.* I have shown Luther hesitating for more than ten years on this question and publishing only in August of 1530 his small work: *Withdrawal from Purgatory.*

Yet, if Luther was followed on this point by all the Protestant Churches, it is certain that neither he nor the great leaders of the Protestant Churches of his time had any doubt about the eternity of the punishments of hell as about the eternity of the joys of heaven.

Very recently, among us, a voice was raised in favor of "universal re-establishment," and, more precisely, in favor of the final conversion of Satan. That voice is from the converted novelist Giovanni Papini, in *The Devil*, a book which I have before my eyes and which has just been translated into French. I must say, in truth, that neither the historians nor the theologians among us took it seriously. The former raised their eyebrows before the numerous inexactitudes of fact; and the latter, startled by continual paradoxes, often on the verge of extravagance, limited themselves to saying: "He is a poet, he is an artist, he is a novelist. Let us smile and let us pass on!"

The book has not, therefore, been condemned and without doubt will not be. For what good? However, the thesis which he maintains has no chance of being admitted in the Catholic Church, whose doctrine has been established once for all in this matter as in all others.

That will be just one of the points that we will have to debate fraternally, in our next letters: namely, this immutability of Catholic doctrine paralleled by the "variations" of the Protestant Churches.

What I would like to say, first of all, is that I find it astonishing and sad—pardon this word—that, after your Churches rejected for powerful reasons the doctrine of predestination (as taught by Luther and Calvin, and therefore a doctrine essentially founded on the negation of free will) no one was found in the bosom of your Churches to draw the logical consequences of this rejection. The negation of free will was, for Luther and Calvin, the essential pivot. With this pivot disappearing, it would have been necessary to build a new machine from all the other points of Faith. Since man is free and cooperates with grace, it is impossible for him not to

have merits in good works, and degrees in the free cooperation with grace, and stages in the sanctity so obtained, and,
consequently, differences in the destinies beyond the grave.
It is from all this complexity of ideas that our teaching on
paradise, purgatory and hell flows.

It seems to me that what the negation of purgatory has
most seriously—and, in our eyes, most regrettably—caused
is the abandonment of prayers for the dead. These prayers are
an important part of Catholic piety. Knowing that our
prayers can lighten the pains of purgatory, knowing on the
other hand that, according to the word of St. Paul, "charity
does not die," and that the souls in purgatory, gifted with
love, pray also for us, there is thus created between us and
our dead, bonds of a very powerful and very consoling Christian fraternity. Let it suffice to have indicated that here.

I believe that I detect, in the last part of your letter, an
invitation to express my sentiments on "the Inquisition, St.
Bartholomew's, the Revocation of the Edict of Nantes, and
the Dragonnades."

I feel no embarrassment in doing so.

We have just lost among the clergy of Lyons a zealous
priest who spent a part of his life in establishing more trusting
and more comprehensive relations between the Catholic and
the Protestant Churches. Undoubtedly, you know his name:
the Abbé Couturier. He persuaded himself that the high
ecclesiastical French authorities could take a decisive step in
the reunion of Churches if they publicly formulated a solemn
disavowal of St. Bartholomew's and of the Revocation of the
Edict of Nantes. He would have desired that, at the least, the
Primate of Gaul, the Archbishop of Lyons, would proclaim
this disavowal. Consulted on this subject, I replied that the
union of the Churches could not be subordinated solely to
such a disavowal; that in addition, there was question of
facts of the political order, in which the Church of France
as such could have nothing to disavow. I am still of the same

opinion. I consider, as a historian, that we are no more linked, insofar as we are Catholics, to St. Bartholomew's or to the Revocation of the Edict of Nantes, than M. René Coty, the actual head of the French state, feels himself identified with Catherine de Medici, the main one responsible for St. Bartholomew's; or with Louis XIV, who was responsible for the Revocation of the Edict of Nantes, although M. Coty is the successor, at one and the same time, of Charles IX and of Louis XIV. If it be necessary to utter a disavowal, I shall willingly do so here, as far as I am allowed to speak in the name of my Church. Not only do we regret and condemn these acts—and especially the unspeakable Dragonnades— as much as Protestants, but we censure and despise them more than they; for, in our opinion, hangmen are always more despicable than the victims; and, in fact, either blinded by passion (as in the case of St. Bartholomew's) or deceived by false rumors and political illusions (as in the case of the Revocation), the executioners were Catholics and their victims were Protestants. I am sure that on your side, you condemn and regret with equal vehemence the too numerous persecutions, the victims of which we honor as martyrs of the Faith.

Let us desire that these horrors be not renewed. There are, alas! sufficient others, under our own eyes, to take their place.

Kindly accept, dear Pastor, my very respectful sentiments in our Lord.

L. CRISTIANI

VIII

† / †

"I Believe in the Holy Spirit . . . the Church"

15.

Dear Canon Cristiani,

In the haste of writing and explaining to you our way of living the *Credo*, it has happened that some of my letters were dispatched before your reply to the preceding one reached me. Hence, there is a certain disorder in our correspondence for which I am to blame. You will certainly make the necessary allowance: the rhythm of the modern pastorate, broken up by telephone calls and unforeseen interviews, lends itself with difficulty to a sustained effort. One must grasp one's pen, make use of it and abuse it, when time permits. Over and above that, our intention to devote ourselves to the commentary of the Apostles' Creed allows a relative independence in writing. The problem of the Church will check me: we are arriving now at the heart of the difficulty, and it is necessary to proceed more systematically.

From your preceding letters one or two points still merit a brief supplementation.

On the question of predestination in St. Augustine—as

on the explanation of every difficult author—interpreters are in disagreement. For my part, I adopt the explanation of Msgr. Duchesne, who summarizes the Bishop of Hippo as follows: "According to him [St. Augustine], free will had no initiative in the work of salvation" (*Ancient History of the Church*, III, 274). He justifies his reason in the commentaries to which I refer you. Such a gauge is certainly Catholic.

On the cult of images I must make a reservation: between putting a crucifix in a sanctuary and venerating images the distance is enormous. Do not ask me to elaborate any further!

I admit much more willingly the catholicity of intention which you attribute to me. To be considered as brothers—is that not to admit implicity that we belong to the same Church? As regards baptism, we have the same concept as you, and we never rebaptize. Can the Father, the Son and the Holy Spirit be other at Rome than at Geneva, other at Wittenberg than at Canterbury and Athens? Baptism, even in our separation, remains a visible sign of unity. Moreover, we say of a Catholic imbued with the spirit of Jesus Christ, "He also is a true Christian." Your propositions recall to mind the emotion raised among us when the Bishop of Fribourg, the late Msgr. Besson, treated us as "parishioners outside the walls." And why not? I prefer that terminology to that of Canon Law, which speaks about us, in connection with mixed marriages, as "a danger of perversion!" If you annex us so amicably, it would be better for us to do the same rather than get angry! It is by fraternity avowed and lived in mutual esteem and prayer that we shall discover one day the road leading to one visible Church.

As regards the sacraments, you underline our differences of doctrine and of number. It appears to me difficult to do more than to note it. Like yourself, I also place this problem in its dependence on ecclesiastical organization. You will allow me, surely, a remark and two anecdotes which I hope will not scandalize you too much. Were our ancestors right in showing themselves so meticulous on the nature and the form of the Presence of Christ? Some years ago I was called to the bedside of an aged woman whose itinerary was rather curious: born and baptized a Roman Catholic, she had, at the age of fifteen, followed her father in enrolling in the schismatic church of Père Hyacinthe, married a Swiss-German Protestant at the age of twenty, and joined our Church. She begged me to bring Holy Communion to her but, before taking it, she confided to me a scruple which was running through her weary head: "I believe in the Real Presence," she told me, "in Christ inserted in the Sacrament. Do you authorize me to have Communion in this persuasion?" A catechetical explanation, a doctrinal insistence seemed to me to be highly out of place. "You will communicate according to your belief, I according to mine," I answered. The sober ceremony took place peacefully, and I had the impression that Christ was really present for her as for me.

One of my parishioners to whom I described our correspondence, told me the other day of a similar case. Zwinglian by origin, she had made her first Communion in the Lutheran Church in Rumania, the only one where German, her maternal tongue, was spoken. She entered into a lively discussion with her pastor about the Sacrament, identical with that which separated Luther from Zwingli. "*Es ist* (this is)," insisted the pastor, an ardent follower of consubstantiation; "*es bedeutet* (that means)," replied the young Swiss girl, faithful to the conviction of her early infancy. Finally, the clergyman, who could not doubt the sincerity and the seriousness of her faith, ended exactly with the same solution as in my first story.

If I cite to you these experiences which are genuine, it is because I see the route of harmony, apart from them, with difficulty. "Receive him who is weak into the Faith and do not argue over opinions," St. Paul counsels (Rom. 14:1). Is it not the secular fault of your Church as of mine to have forgotten this exhortation? Oh, I realize there is the danger of relativism, but is it not less destructive than that provoked by secular disputes? Pardon me for saying this so rudely and so bluntly! It is a conviction which keeps growing in my heart. "And from the abundance of the heart the mouth speaketh!" The scandal of the separated communions which the Ecumenical Assembly in Amsterdam experienced makes the problem a fiery one in the very bosom of non-Catholic Churches.

Let us turn from there to the essential problem of the Church itself. By a compelling coincidence my letter will leave Zurich tonight, July 16. On July 16, 1054, exactly nine hundred years ago, the Legate of Pope Leo IX, Cardinal Humbert of Moyenmoutier, flanked by Chancellor Frederick of Lorraine, placed on the altar of Saint Sophia a verdict of excommunication directed against the Patriarch of Constantinople, Michael Cerularius. A copy of the Bull was solemnly burnt some days later, a far-off prelude to the burning in effigy of Wittenberg.

If the Church is infallible, this double schism sorrowfully places in jeopardy the wisdom of its directors. Could not they in both cases have shown patience and discussed it quietly? Each of these two crises took place amid a very human tension, far too human.

But, before having recourse to the main texts of the Gospels on the foundation of the Church, permit me, aside from all polemics, though in a positive manner, to present to you the development of my Protestant exegesis on the Apostles' Creed.

The third part of the *Credo* concerns the Holy Spirit. The question that presents itself is to know whether the realities enumerated in succession, all of which partake more or less of the invisible—namely, the holy universal Church, the communion of saints, the remission of sins, the resurrection of the body, and life everlasting—are related uniquely to the Holy Spirit.

Are not God and Christ the authors of pardon and of the new life, as well as the Holy Spirit? We are ascertaining here the Unity of the Three Persons. Christ and the Holy Spirit are God, are the presence of God. What the Holy Spirit produces, God and Christ also produce! With the same God, Christ and the Holy Spirit are all together in the work of creation and redemption. Theologians express this when they say, "External works are indivisible." The Church and the realities mentioned in order are, then, the common work of the Three Divine Persons.

More delicate is the distinction between "I believe in the Holy Spirit" and "I believe in the Holy Church," which introduce the last words. Protestants find here a sort of break. The Holy Spirit is part of the Trinity. He is the object of Faith, being God, because he is God. On the other hand, one does not believe in the Church: this is a work of the Trinity, like creation and the Resurrection. One of our ancient catechisms, that of Cellerier (1845), expresses it rather well: "We say: I believe the holy universal catholic Church and not *in* the holy Church, nor *through* the holy Church, because the last expressions would represent an act of faith similar to that which is directed towards God, the Father, the Son and the Holy Spirit; an act of recourse, of confidence, of love which can be offered only to the Divinity."

The Holy Spirit, if we study the sense of the term in the Bible, is God present in the hearts of men, guiding them, consoling them, sanctifying them. In the Old Testament, if He is already acting in creation (Gen. 1:2), He abides in the leaders, the kings, and the prophets; He has devolved on only a few. However, the time will come, they believe, when He will be extended over all creatures. Christ Himself received the Holy Spirit at His baptism, as a new mark of His essential unity with the Father. Through the Christ-Man the Holy

Spirit will be given in abundance to other men, His disciples. The Church, from this viewpoint, appears, in the first place, as a fruit of the Spirit in such wise that, despite the caution made above, it is normal that the *Credo* binds them closely together.

The Holy Spirit—God and Christ among us, one might say —works here below, invisible and present in a multitude of souls. He is that power which lifts them above themselves, which gives them wisdom and love, which combats the sloth in them and permits them to radiate forth. The Holy Spirit has written His presence in those vast archives of the people of God: the Bible. The pages of the Bible pulsate with the breath of the Spirit. Those profound words, those acts of courage, that hope which decimates despair, are born of Him. To read the Bible is to encounter the Spirit, so that Saint Paul could write: "The whole of Scripture is inspired by God and useful to teach, to conquer, to correct, to instruct in justice, that the man of God be accomplished, and furnished to every good work" (II Tim. 3:16).

You know what importance Protestantism, since its beginning, has attached to the Bible: translations, commentaries, catechisms, sermons based on a text of the Scripture. It is the bedside book of our faithful, because it is the book of the Holy Spirit. In this respect, the discussions of the nineteenth century ending on the authenticity of the texts precipitated a whole generation into a veritable nightmare. "Is what instructs us, aids us, inspires us, only a mass of human tradition without value?" they keep on wondering. The reply came little by little through the lacerating of many a pastoral conscience. The Bible is the book of the Spirit, but the Spirit is not to be confused with the letter. St. Paul already taught: "The letter kills, but the spirit vivifies" (II Cor. 3:6). The Spirit is a living breath and His redemptive passage does not depend upon a literal, slavish interpretation. Thus, the six days of Genesis can represent six stages of a thousand, a hundred thousand or of a hundred million years without the value of the revelation "God is the author of everything" being lessened. The more frequent perusal of the Scriptures by Catholics brings us immense joy: that common fervor will surely bring together one day the dispersed fragments of Christianity. Drinking from the same source, meditating on the same texts, how could these not produce in us the same fruits? Yet the Spirit does not isolate Himself in ancient accounts. Whenever He passes, consciences awake to become in their turn messengers of life. A multitude of witnesses bear testimony of God and communicate their faith to us. Is it not St. Paul who compares believers to "letters of Christ written, not with ink, but with the Spirit of the Living God" (II Cor. 3:3)? If I look back and seek to discover the origin of my Faith, I find about me a wreath of venerable faces, men and women whose prayers, counsels and example were my guide. What thus passes from one Christian to another is the Spirit. The latter gives to the former exactly that which elevates him above himself, what Jesus Christ and the Spirit have written "not on tablets of stone, but on the tablets of the flesh, on hearts."

In this respect, the Spirit and the Church are intimately linked, as we have seen. The uproarious debates of the sixteenth century have often hidden to Catholics the fact that Protestants professed the *holy* and *universal Church*. Open, for example, *The Apology of the Profession of Augsburg* by Melancthon; it affirms that the Church is "The Living Body of Christ, not only in name, but also in reality, and that it is a communion which is not satisfied with exterior signs, but where each will possess the Holy Spirit and Faith in his heart" (Roehrich's translation). *The Swiss Confession* of 1566 also insists on the reality of the Church, that is to say, "an assembly of faithful called or gathered from the whole world."

If Protestantism believes the Church, I shall not surprise you, Reverend dear Canon, in affirming that it considers the

Church differently from you. If we were to content ourselves here with a swift and pleasing exposition, we could pass over our secular quarrel in favour of a verbal analogy. This would be to abandon the loyalty which we have mutually promised. Besides, we knew that we were expected, on this occasion, to come up against the problems raised in our first letters.

In this, I doubt, in any event, that I shall be able to summarize our whole thought. I shall give only the first parts of it. The word "Church," from the Greek "ecclesia," which the Latin has literally assumed, possesses in the colloquial the sense of an assembly regularly called together. In the Old Testament, then in the New, the Church is consequently the group of believers, those whom Christ and the Spirit called from the ends of the earth to form one same body. (See the *Biblical Vocabulary* of Belachaux et Niestle.) While in the Old Covenant this assembly is confused with racial belonging, in the New Covenant the Semitic framework is smashed. What the Prophet Osee already predicted: "I shall call my people those who are not my people, and shall call Beloved the nation which was not beloved" (Rom. 9:25; cf. Osee 2:1, 25), is now accomplished. "Men from every tribe, from every tongue, from every people and from every nation," as the Apocalypse says, will recognize one another as brothers and partakers of the same faith. In this sense the Church is "catholic," that is to say, universal; and the Protestants subscribe fully to these terms of the *Credo*: it includes whoever believes in Jesus Christ, wherever he is, or wherever he lives. The fact that Protestants are organized under the form of national Churches has never prevented them from believing in the universality of the Church; one lived in England, the other in Germany, the third in France or in Japan; they knew they were brothers in the faith. On this subject read the correspondence of the Reformers themselves; it is eloquent. Nearer to our own times, study the history of our missions, or that of the very recent Ecumenical Movement; you will see, if I dare use this verbal paradox, to what a point Protestantism is catholic. Truly, it knows no boundary. It is to the credit of a man like the Lutheran Archbishop Soederblom that he thought, before the threat of a growing international tension, that this unity merited to be affirmed in a visible organization. In 1925 he convoked the Conference of Stockholm. His invitation brought together not only ecclesiastics from the four corners of the universe, but also those belonging to different denominations, Presbyterians, Lutherans, Anglicans, and Orthodox. Soederblom, of whom Professor Jean Hoffman has given us an interesting biography in French, did not believe in the possibility of an immediate reunion of the different Churches. In the sight of the world, however, his convocation attests to the spiritual kinship of all those who claim the name of Jesus Christ. He desired that all communicate together. At Lausanne, where he professed that "the free access to the Lord's Supper is one of the best ways of hastening the reconciliation of the Churches," this bold declaration surprised the Anglicans of the extreme right, who opposed it violently. Nevertheless, the movement continued: Oxford and Edinburgh in 1937, Amsterdam in 1948, and in a few days Evanston—all witness its vitality. We regret deeply that the Church of Rome never accepted officially to associate herself with it, and has been content to send observers to the conferences. The Church universal is holy, which means that God is working in her, that the holiness of Jesus Christ urges imitation, that the yeast is penetrating the dough. Protestants ignore the process of canonization; sanctity does not appear to demand an official elevation; but the martyrs, the great Doctors, the defenders of noble causes, and inexhaustible devotions swarm in their ranks, and the memory of exemplary believers is surrounded with deep respect. The multitude of recent biographies is proof in itself: the lives of Josephine Butler, who battled zealously against organized prostitution; Mathilde Wreds, the friend of prisoners; Felix Nef, the fiery evangelist of the Higher Alps; William and Catherine Booth, the founders of the Salvation Army; Albert Schweitzer, the doctor with a great heart who quit his Chair of Theology for a lost corner of Africa. If one goes back to the heroic age of the persecutions, it suffices to open the oft-reedited *History of the Martyrs* by Crespin, who retraces the dramatic submissions of the sixteenth century. Oh, I do not mean to say that all Protestants are saints; far from it! I know only too well our deficiencies and our infidelities, but I believe just as strongly that the Holy Spirit works among us. In this regard, it seems to me that between you and us lies this difference: namely, that Protestant sanctity is more worldly than Catholic sanctity in such wise that our best believers are kin to St. Vincent de Paul rather than to St. Thérèse of Lisieux.

What I am explaining here is the life of our Churches, not their theology. Haunted by the fear of promoting our pride, our dogmaticians—thus, in this generation, Karl Barth—have often insisted on the misery of man to such a point that the work of God in him has been obscured. It is sufficient to consult a text like the *Swiss Confession of 1566* published by Bullinger, the successor of Zwingli, to measure the importance accorded to submission to Christ and to the accomplishment of good works. "We ought to do good works," he specifies, "not to merit eternal life, which is, as the Apostle says, a gift of God; neither for display . . . nor for love of gain and profit . . . but for the glory of God, rendering our vocation honorable, and not showing ourselves ungrateful towards God —and also for the love of the neighbor." Bullinger insists on the phrase: "The good tree brings forth good fruits." He recalls the text of Paul affirming that Christ has given Himself for us in order to redeem us from all iniquity, and to make for "Himself a people who belongs to Him, purified by Him and zealous for good works" (Tit. 2:14): "We condemn those, then, who scorn good works and pretend they are useless." However, it is not the works which save, it is grace

(Eph. 2:8). And the same Bullinger recalls the famous text of Saint Luke (Lk. 7:10): "When you have done all that is commanded of you, say: 'We are ungrateful servants.'"

This fear of pride has led several of ours—and the best—to an extreme discretion in their religious life and devotion. I wish to give here only one example. A few years ago there died in this city at an advanced age an old maid, who, an only daughter, had, since her fortieth year, dedicated herself completely to the housing of children of divorced parents. She received them into her home with maternal solicitude, and gratuitously; for if she demanded an allowance from certain parents, the money placed in a savings account was given back to her protégés on their coming of age. She worked thus without fuss, left all her fortune to a foundation destined to carry on her work, and forbade that this act be made public. No newspaper spoke of it, and I would have been unaware of it if chance had not put me in relation with the executor of her will.

I am a little embarrassed to tell you such things but the aim of these letters is not only to analyze the *Credo* intellectually, but to show the certitudes to which it refers, working in the souls of Protestants. I know that they inspire as well the lives of your co-religionists; and while rejoicing in the thought of hearing from you, I here conclude this exposition, reserving to a new missive what concerns the external form of the Church and its development in time.

Kindly accept, my dear Canon, the expression of my devoted sentiments in our Lord.

JEAN RILLIET

16.

Reverend and dear Pastor,

Here we are, then, at the crucial points of our fraternal debate. You will agree with me that here we must redouble charity as well as clarity. I shall not discuss your points of view. We are not wrangling against each other as was done for too long without any other result than creating confusion and animosity between the Churches, as Cardinal Cajetan had already said in a very sad tone of voice to Luther at the time of the interview at Augsburg in October 1518.

At the utmost, it is not a question of what we think, we poor human beings, about these huge problems which both unite and divide us: the Holy Spirit and His action in Christianity; the Church and her divine institution; the Bible and the importance that it must have in our religious life.

No, on all that, it is Christ whom we must consult; it is He to whom we must go humbly and with love, to ask Him what He wanted to say and do and what He said and did historically.

Following your example, then, in the present letter I shall enter upon the question of the Holy Spirit, the foundation of the Church and the mission which was imposed upon her, and the distinguished role of Holy Scripture in Christian life.

But it seems to me that these momentous things ought to be, before all, placed "in their context" carefully.

I consider "context," here, what we have already said and what we know and believe of Christ. He is, we have said in repeating His own words, "The Way, the Truth, and the Life." He was the visible expression of infinite love which is God Himself, in His Holy Trinity. He could act only in the direction of His being, that is, in the line of His love for His Father and for us. That is what I meant, in an earlier letter, when recalling that the most perfect *logic* could not stop existing for a single instant in the work of the divine *Logos*. Who would then be logical if the *Logos* were not?

This is also what our inimitable and great Charles Péguy wanted to say in his deliberately droll manner, in this passage from his works:

"Jesus Christ, my child,
did not come to tell us fairy tales . . .
He did not make the voyage to come down on earth
To come to tell us funny stories,
And fibs . . .
He did not put, He did not use, He did not spend all that,
His thirty years of work and His three years of preaching
    and His three days of passion and death . . .
To come afterwards and pour out nonsense . . .
Riddles,
To be guessed,
As though He were a fortune teller.
Jesus Christ, my child, did not give us words as preserves
To keep,
But He gave us living words
To nourish us.
"I am the Way, the Truth and the Life."
(See the whole moving passage in *Le Porche du Mystère de la Deuxième Vertu*.)

"Living words"; that is, a living and speaking Church, under the direction of the Holy Spirit; such is the Catholic thesis.

"Words for preserves"; that is, the Bible left to the free scrutiny of men; such, unless I am mistaken, is the Protestant thesis.

Let us examine in detail what is in our Gospels.

In the first place: the Holy Spirit. On three occasions in

the discourse after the Last Supper in St. John, Jesus promised us the Holy Spirit. The first time (14:15–17), He names Him the Paraclete, that is, the Defender, the Advocate and, more clearly still, the Spirit of *truth* "which the world cannot receive because it does not see Him and does not know Him. As for you," adds Jesus, "you know Him because He lives in you and He is in you."

The second time (14:25–26), He explains Himself more clearly still: "I have said these things while I was living near you. But the Defender, the Holy Spirit, whom my Father will send in my name, is he who will teach you and who will recall to your memory all that I have said."

The third time, Jesus declares that He is going away only to send to us the Paraclete, or Defender, who "will show the world its errors," because "the prince of this world is already judged." And he concludes: "I have still many things to say to you but you are not in a condition to bear them now. But when he shall have come, the Spirit of truth, *he will guide* you towards the whole truth . . ."

Here then is a first point of blinding clarity for you and for me, the function of the Holy Spirit—to guide us toward the whole truth.

Here the question of Pilate may present itself: "What is truth?" It seems to me that in contemplating the astonishing diversity of opinions which separated the Catholics from the Protestants, face to face with the Bible, and Protestants among themselves for four centuries, one is indeed forced to wonder "What is truth?" Would it be the totality of opinions, of which each one would be only an aspect of this very entire truth? Or rather does there exist one truth, unique, absolute, in opposition to all the wavering opinions of men, in which it is necessary to see only errors, either partial or complete?

I believe that one would indeed have astonished all those who lived, reasoned and disputed before Hegel, by telling them that truth could exist, if not simultaneously, at least successively, in contradictory statements. Neither Luther nor Calvin admitted two truths. They believed that *their* truth was that of Jesus Christ, and that it excluded all the others. It seems to me that St. Paul has well expressed what we ought to admit about truth in the teaching of Christ when he wrote to the Corinthians (II, 1:18–20): "God is my witness that our message to you is not both 'Yes' and 'No.' For the Son of God, Jesus Christ, who was preached among you by us . . . was not now 'Yes' and now 'No,' but only 'Yes' was in him. For all the promises of God find their 'Yes' in him; and therefore through him also rises the 'Amen' to God unto our glory. . . ."

In the face of truth, then, we have only one word to say: Amen. Jesus Christ Himself gives us a teaching, clear, precise, definitive, where there is no place for "yes" and "no," but only for "yes."

That being established, what means did Jesus Christ take in order that, under the inspiration of the Holy Spirit, the "yes" should come to us with such preciseness and sureness that we would have to say no more than this single word of acquiescence and of faith: Amen!

Assuredly, one could admit, as Calvin did after Luther, that Jesus Christ had foreseen as an infallible means the Bible alone.

In order that this solution be possible, it would have been necessary that Jesus Christ assure us of it, that He tell it to us openly, that He promise the Holy Spirit, not to His whole church, but to each reader of the Bible.

Here we can divide the problem. The Bible contains two parts, the Old and the New Testament. The Old is only a prelude, a preparation for the New; an outline, a sketch before the final painting. Had we been left with only the Old Testament, we would still be Jews and not Christians. Is that what Jesus Christ wanted? Surely not. He has well said:

"Examine the Scriptures, they are those which speak of me," but He knew well that it would be especially the doctrine preached by Himself and, after that, by His apostles, which would reveal Him Himself and the whole truth, in view of our salvation, redeemed by His passion and His death. You and I, we are indeed in agreement on this point, that it is not in the Old Testament but solely in the New that it is necessary to search for that redemptive truth.

What, then, has our Lord done to transmit this unique truth to us? I always return to the same question: "What has Jesus done who is the Way, the Truth and the Life, in order that the Way be always open before men, the Truth always proposed without equivocation or doubt, the Life communicated by definite means?"

If he had wanted above all to give us a *book*, should He not either have written it Himself or dictated it or, at least, given an order to His apostles to write it, after His death? Otherwise there will always remain a doubt in the minds of even Christian critics. I think of Harnack declaring after the demonstrations of Batiffol: "These demonstrations would be final if there did not always exist an uncrossable ditch between the thought of Jesus Christ, between what He said and taught, and what the apostles afterwards learned, retained and reported about Him."

At the utmost, didn't Jesus Christ have before His eyes, before His eyes as a Man who knows men—without calling upon His infallible science as God—the spectacle of the Bible left in the hands of the Jews? Sadducees and Pharisees quarreled about it, never agreed either on the Canon of the Scriptures or on the sense of the texts. If the Pharisees were nearer to the "Biblical truth" than the Saducees, had our Lord approved, in the least, the spirit in which they read and explained the Scriptures? Was it simple prudence on the part of a man—I do not say a genius, much less a God-Man—to leave the Scriptures, those existing as well as those which apostolic writers would add to them, to the free discussions of men?

I will summarize my thought: neither did Jesus Christ write the Bible nor did He ask that it be written. The texts which form our New Testament are therefore very sacred writings, but nonetheless occasional writings, discontinued, answering particular needs, and drawing their durable and immortal value from the fact that the living Church, created by Jesus Christ, has adopted them, recognizing them as inspired and conforming to the Faith of which she had the deposit and which she alone, among the discussions which even sacred texts can never fail to occasion amongst men, would have the right and the duty to explain, to comment on, to define the meaning which they must have for us.

The most natural reasoning should therefore lead us to this conclusion: Jesus Christ has transmitted to us the Way, the Truth and the Life, under the guarantee of His Holy Spirit, through an indefectible and infallible Church. For this Church to be "the column and the foundation of the truth," as St. Paul defines it in his first epistle to Timothy (3:15), it had to be one visible Church, having official organs, so that one would know where to address oneself, and, consequently, a saintly hierarchy, formed undoubtedly of men, but of men representing God Himself.

Thus I understand all the acts by which Jesus Christ prepared and then founded His Church. I understand that, from the beginning, he separated the Twelve, then gave them a chief in the person of Peter. And I should add in passing that I cannot believe, with the scholarly M. Cullman, one of your most remarkable historians today, that this title of chief was given only to Peter, and that temporarily! Did Jesus Christ, the God-Man, ignore that His Church would have an even greater need for a leader in the long sequence of ages that was just beginning? But let us close this parenthesis. The words of Christ to Peter: "Thou art Peter, and on this rock I shall build my Church, and the gates of hell will not prevail against it," and also: "Feed my sheep, feed my lambs," and also: "Confirm your brothers"—these words, I say, are not words said for a day, for a generation, for a century, but for the whole sequence of centuries right down to the end of time, just as the foundation of an immortal edifice must last as long as the edifice itself, in such a way that it could not disappear except after the disappearance of the edifice itself.

To conclude: it is in this great context of infinite love that I read these words which you read yourself in the last page of Matthew's Gospel: "All power has been given me in heaven and on earth. Go, therefore, and teach all nations, baptizing them in the name of the Father, the Son and the Holy Ghost. Teach them to keep all my commandments. As for myself, I am with you all days until the end of time."

If these words do not signify the definite foundation of the Church, announced and prepared, if they do not herald an indefectible and infallible Church, a visible and hierarchic Church, I confess that I understand nothing more from the texts or the lessons of history.

I know that the concept of an authoritative Church shocks many minds among you. That is why there would be a great advantage in discussing it in our next letter.

Kindly accept, Reverend and dear Pastor, my very respectful sentiments in our Lord.

L. CRISTIANI

IX

† / †

Church, Scripture, Tradition

17.

Dear Canon Cristiani,

The further we progress in these epistolary interviews, the more I am fascinated by the possibility which is granted us of confronting our convictions in a friendly way! However, our discussion is not wholly unimpassioned. It occurred to me to reread the letters which we have exchanged: I sense in you, just as in myself, the fire of conviction. If the twentieth century has its defects, in religious matters at least, it grants us a living and sincere contact.

I am doing a great deal of reading while writing these letters to you, particularly the Fathers of the Church. I have reopened these days, Irenaeus, Tertullian, St. Cyprian, a few among the most ancient authors of this Latin Church to which we are both attached.

In his *Contra Omnes Haereses*, there is nothing more edifying than the way in which the Bishop of Lyons underlines the unity of Scripture and that of Tradition. At Rome, He describes the succession of the first Bishops of Rome who transmitted to each other the torch of the Faith from Peter right down to his own time: Linus, Anacletus, Clement, Evaristus, Alexander, Sixtus, Telephorus (a glorious martyr), and finally Hyginus, Pius and Anicetus, ten men who, since Peter, have led the destinies of the diocese. In Asia Minor there exists the same continuity; Irenaeus, who was brought up there, recalls the memory of Polycarp, an essential link in the chain which binds him to the apostles; Irenaeus, while still young, was well acquainted with the eminent old man and had heard him speak of St. John, whose disciple he had been. A few more steps and the tradition reaches back to the Twelve: Anicetus and Irenaeus almost reach back to them. Hence, one can well understand why the pious writer exalts the value of this oral transmission: "If the apostles had not left the Scriptures to us, should we not then follow the order of the tradition which they have transmitted to those to whom they entrusted the Churches" (III, 4)? *"Si neque apostoli quidem scripturas reliquissent nobis"*—If the Scriptures had not existed, there would be Tradition. Irenaeus refers in this regard to the barbarians, the unbelievers, who possess the salvation of Christ "written in their hearts by the Spirit without ink and without paper, *sine charta et atramento.*" In the rest of the volume he points out, against the monstrous heresies of Valentine, of Cerinthus and of the Ophites, the complete unity of Tradition and Scripture. In the face of those who believe in the existence of two Gods, one who is the author of evil and the other the author of good, or also in two Christs, one who died on the Cross and the other who escaped out of that valueless body and went up to heaven directly, there is only one Christianity. It suffices to read your letters and mine to see that, united with Irenaeus and with Scripture and Tradition, we would still reject today with great energy the absurd wanderings of the Gnostics.

You know that our disagreements are of a different kind.

The big question asked by the sixteenth century was in fact this: between the Church of the second century, that of Irenaeus, and the Church of Leo X, was there not a slow modification? Did not ecclesiastical customs and doctrines suffer an evolution which rendered the Catholic Church on certain points a stranger to the ancient Church? Thus, in the New Testament, we find neither the prayers for the dead nor the cult of the saints nor the immense role of the Virgin nor pontifical infallibility. That perfect agreement between the Scriptures and Tradition which is for Irenaeus the object of no doubt whatever, does it still exist?

The actual Catholic historians are unanimous in admitting that during the Middle Ages, and this on more than one occasion, the papacy had gone through serious moral crises. The disorders of the Renaissance are notorious. On the less known period which extends from St. Gregory the Great to the year 1000, it is enough to read the details given by an impartial historian such as M. Daniel-Rops. Obviously, the head of the Church is ill: queer pontiffs such as the weak Hadrian II, the intriguing Formosus, Stephen VI, who died strangled in his bed—these in no way recall the saintly bishops of the first two centuries. John XII, "that child invested with the tiara," about whom public rumour spread stories of carousing orgies, put even Alexander Borgia to shame. (See *The Church of the Barbaric Ages*, p. 641.) A reform was necessary, and, thank God, it was accomplished! Where did it come from? From the convents and the hermitages where a multitude of saints, such as Odon, Maisul, Odilon, Hugues, Romuald, Peter Damien, are passionately seeking God. From them, the spirit of reformation reaches Rome and, with men like Silvester II and his successors, sweeps away at least certain abuses.

It is sufficient to read such a story attentively, to realize that the moral transformation necessary originated in the body of the Church, spreading till it reached its head. The

part of a St. Bernard, who, a century later, berates the
court of Rome, confirms this thesis. It is not the papacy, but
the Holy Spirit who has saved the Church. The crisis is overcome; the promise of Christ is accomplished: "The gates of
hell shall not prevail against it." You know that Protestant
historians maintain, whether rightly or wrongly, a similar
thesis for the sixteenth century; the criticism directed by the
very Reformers whom she was rejecting caused consciences
in the Church herself to be stirred. The service rendered to
Catholicism by Luther would be that of forcing her to break
from the disorders of the Renaissance.

In conclusion, a distinction seems necessary between the
Church as a social reality, and the Church as the Mystical
Body of Jesus Christ.

The Church, as a social reality, is a people recruited by
Baptism with its numbers and its heads. It includes all those
who participate, more or less assiduously, in her ritual life.
In practice, birth makes a Christian. Italians, Frenchmen, or
Germans since the end of paganism till the birth of free
thought are automatically incorporated into the ranks of the
baptized. But, in the bosom of this vast community, the
Spirit, in accordance with the word of our Lord, breathes
where He wills. He is not attached to one part of that mass;
He animates it; He vivifies it through personalities whose
role and actions remain unforeseeable. I would believe it
wrong to say that there is a Church within the Church. The
boundaries of both groups are as indistinct as is yeast in the
dough. Certainly, the Spirit is not to be confused with the
hierarchy; some of those who, in your Church today, are fac-
tors of life have occupied positions of very little importance.
Think of Pascal, the holy Curé d'Ars, Frederick Ozanam. Is
not the expression of Strohl, already quoted, "the apostolic
succession of the faithful," arresting in its truth? Although
the Reformers were speaking of the invisible Church, the expression leads to confusion, because those who have been in

our Churches, in yours as well as mine, instruments of the Holy Spirit, are very real Christians, even though they occupied positions of little importance.

These thoughts will appear to you terribly Protestant. They summarize a concept of the Church which I doubt you can ever accept, but they will show you to what point we think seriously of the duration and the continuity of the Church. The difference which exists between us is, hence, easily perceptible: while you conceive of the Church as a society constantly in progress, with a doctrine which becomes ceaselessly more definite and an organization always more perfect, we conceive of it as a reality, human and divine at the same time, human by its misery, its disobediences, its slowness, its errors, divine by the presence in it of the yeast of the Holy Spirit, who takes it in hand, raises it up again, and ceaselessly causes new devoutness, prophets and saints. And in these awakenings of the faith, the Bible, that living book, plays its part. The Spirit uses it, especially the Gospels, to change hearts. Its principal part is in keeping a reserve of truth which the Paraclete uses to lead, in each generation, attentive men in the way *of all truth.*

You quote in your last letter the admirable volume of M. Oscar Cullman, *Peter: Disciple, Apostle, Martyr,* which facilitates my task considerably, because I can refer you back to it for a number of details. The eminent exegete rejects the doubtful procedure employed by a whole group of Protestant critics at the end of the last century who rejected the famous text: "You are Peter and on this rock I shall build my Church" (Matt. 16:18), by saying that it was not authentic. This verse, according to M. Cullman, could not possibly be the later addition of an editor. Jesus has willed His Church and that through Peter's action. On reading an account of Pentecost where the Apostle is the mouthpiece of the Twelve and where his sermon converts thousands of Israelites, we see that the prophecy of Christ is accomplished with a particular brilliance. But this phrase, M. Cullman notes, concerns Peter: nowhere is there a question of his successors. "The gates of hell will not prevail against it," it is written—a promise relating to the Church in Jerusalem and in Antioch just as in Rome, and without doubt in Geneva just as in Lyons, in Stockholm just as in Canterbury.

The Gospel does not contain a single word about pontifical succession which would insure to Rome alone the privileges of Peter. The latter, according to M. Cullman, has in any event neither governed the Church long, nor especially alone. After a few years in Jerusalem, is it not James who leads the bark of the Church while the Apostle devotes himself entirely to missionary work (*op. cit.*, p. 202)? As for the Roman bishops, if Irenaeus sees in them faithful guardians of Tradition, their claim to the direction of the Church which goes on increasing, soon meets the resistance of men such as Tertullian (*op. cit.*, p. 210) and later, far more energetically, of Firmilian, Bishop of Caesarea, the correspondent and friend of St. Cyprian (see *Letters of St. Cyprian*, 75, 17). You may also have heard of the profound study of patristic texts relative to Peter which the Anglican Canon Moreton has given us in his precious little book published by Fischbacher (1938), which contains several interesting pieces about this important process.

The quotations of the Fathers corroborate the silence of the New Testament. If the institution of the papacy went back to Christ Himself, why has He not defined the part and duration of such an essential organism Himself? The discussions of the Corinthians which St. Paul assails—do they not demonstrate clearly that in the primitive Church there did not exist an infallible magisterium (see I Cor. 1:12–13, 3:4–5). If Peter is the rock on which the Church of Pentecost is raised, has not Paul on the other hand planted the Church of Corinth? "According to the grace which God has given me," he says, "I have laid the foundation like a wise architect" (I Cor. 3:10). This foundation is Jesus Christ (see verse 2). If the Apostle of the Gentiles returns to Jerusalem to consult his elders in the Faith, it is a collective authority —namely, the apostles, the presbyters and the brethren— which brings support to him (Acts 15:23).

But the most astonishing texts which can be opposed to the monarchical theory of the Church adopted by the Middle Ages, are, in my opinion, found in the letters of Pope St. Gregory the Great. In his struggles with John, the ambitious Patriarch of Constantinople, he found lashing replies to beat down the latter's pride. See how he ridicules his pretension of being called Universal Bishop. "Peter," he wrote to the Emperor Maurice Augustus, "received the keys of the kingdom of heaven, the power of binding and loosing; the care of the whole Church and the primacy were given to him and yet he is not called Universal Bishop. However, John, a very holy man and my colleague in the priesthood, attempts to have himself called Universal Bishop. I feel myself compelled to cry out and say: 'O times, O customs!' " "And that," he remarks again, "at the time when Europe is devastated by the barbarians, when cities are destroyed, when castles are overthrown! How dare he, in such conditions, cover himself with 'names of vanity' and glorify himself with new and worldly titles?"

"Certainly," he adds a little further in this letter, "to honor Peter, the Prince of the Apostles, this same title was offered to the Roman Pontiff by the august Council of Chalcedon! But none of them ever wished to make use of this singular title for fear that in giving any particular thing to one, all the other bishops might be deprived of the honor which is due them. In what concerns me," he will write once more with a remarkable modesty, "I am the servant of all the bishops insofar as they live sacerdotally" (Texts in *Letters*, Migne, Patr. Lat. 77, pp. 747–748). Now, what he said to the Emperor he confirms in his letters to his colleagues Eulogius,

Bishop of Alexandria, and Anastasius, Bishop of Antioch: *"Quia videlisset si unus Patriarca universalis dicitur, Patriarcarum nomen ceteris derogatur*—Because, truly, if one is called universal, the others are deprived of the name of Patriarch" (*op. cit.*, p. 771). To the same Eulogius, who praises him for sitting on the Chair of Peter, he recalls that Peter honored three of them, at Rome, at Alexandria, and at Antioch, and he points out the unity of these three bishoprics (*op. cit.*, see *Letter* 40, pp. 898–899). Do not these texts prove incontestably that, before sinking into the darkness of the Middle Ages, Rome, through one of her most illustrious representatives refused again to disassociate her destiny from that of the other patriarchates? And through the mouth of St. Gregory, is it not precious to hear recalled that the worth of the bishop depends, not on his seat or his title, but on the manner in which he lives sacerdotally?

Excuse me for these historical reminiscences, capable of stirring up the flames of a discussion, but they will explain why Protestantism—and Anglicanism with it—terminates in the notion of a fallible Church, applying this term (that goes without saying!) not to the Church as a creation ceaselessly upheld by the Holy Spirit, but to the Church composed of men who have not all equally opened their hearts to the living breath of the Paraclete.

In the experience of human fallibility there are some very painful incidents. We all aspire to perfection. When we have discovered the faults of our immediate environment and that of our own misery, we refer our disappointed desires to the society that surrounds us, some to the State, others to the Church. The more clear-sighted appraisal which reveals the weaknesses of these superb institutions leaves the heart at a loss! But the latter succeeds in better perceiving the work of God in the midst of sinners such as we are. The Gospel is there, an inexhaustible source of pardon and of holiness with Jesus Christ, the Way, the Truth and the Life. Grace labors in souls and slowly lifts some of them above themselves. Who are the saints, if not hearts deeply ploughed by the Father, in whom the living word is better rooted? This transformation is never tied to a function. A part of human fallibility exists, besides, in the best Christian. Recall the cry of faith uttered by Paul, to whom an idolatrous crowd wishes to make a sacrifice: "We also, we are men with the same nature as you" (Acts 14:15). And if the Apostle refuses thus a trust which is ill-placed, how much more ought the Church, instructed by its experience of a thousand years, make itself humble and unassuming—the Church, which is the field of God. "The Lord," it is written at the end of Chapter II of the Acts, "adds each day to the Church those who are saved." The Church, a living reality, increases by conversions. She is built of men. In these conditions, how can one imagine it as a body, completely stranger to our weaknesses, to our hesitations, to our illusions?

You have raised, in a preceding letter, the continuity of a State in its diversity by linking Catherine de Medici to M. René Coty. *Mutatis mutandis*, the Church also varies; she has her ups and downs. Let us underline only this point: she has been democratic in her form in the beginning, as the election of Mathias recalls (Acts 1:23), then monarchical. She counts today one branch—Rome, which remains in the line of Innocent III; another—Canterbury, which is related to constitutional monarchy; another—Geneva, which is Republican. Through all, the Spirit, who acts in the Church through the Gospel, is at work. Yet His presence is not localized either in the Roman Pontiff, or in the Archbishop of Canterbury, or in the Consistory of Geneva. He can breathe on constituted authority, but also bypass it. I do not believe that Christianity enjoys a privilege refused to the kings of Israel and to the Sanhedrin.

Peter was the rock on which the Church of the first century arose. May God grant us many personalities of that stature! If the Church is made up of men, she has the joy of receiving often from the hands of God those who are capable of guiding her and of stirring up about them new enthusiasms. I ask God, for my part, to greet them without sectarianism, wherever He will place them; but I refuse to believe, based on the lesson of the centuries, that they are situated in a single city, even if it be that where Peter died. What ought not to be, then, the privilege of Jerusalem, where our Lord suffered the pains which redeemed us?

Such a subject is inexhaustible. I have tried to define here the Protestant concept of the Church in opposition to that of Catholicism. Was it not necessary to keep our promise of being perfectly frank towards each other? I regret to have had to make use of historical investigations which recall a painful past! But the Protestant reflects on the problem of authority with the shuddering sensitivity of the child who has received blows. He cannot forget his bitter memories. However, I hope that I have lacked neither correctness nor charity and I beg you, my dear Canon, to accept the assurance of my faithful respect in our Lord.

JEAN RILLIET

P.S. I have finally been able to obtain the collection of letters of Luther which you cite in connection with St. Augustine. The argumentation of Melanchthon is displeasing and shows well to what errors the polemic soul can lead one. However, his avowal of a difference between Augustianism and Lutheranism concerns infused justification distinguished from forensic justification. It does not seem to me that my judgment on Augustine's predestination ought to be modified. As for our theologians, Augustine believes in the free will of Adam but refuses it to his descendants. Those constitute a *massa damnata,* a condemned multitude from which God draws whom He wills. Why cite the historians of my belief? I recalled the opinion of Msgr. Duchesne, and it is better still to read the texts themselves; the excellent translation published by Desclée de Brouwer puts them at the disposal of anyone. I am referring you in particular to Volume IX, *Exposés généraux de la Foi*, pp. 153 to 163, and 273 to 293. The commentary of the editor does not appear convincing to me (see pp. 396 to 398).

18.

Reverend and dear Pastor,
It is with great pleasure that I shall follow your lead through history and be careful to adhere to the convention which we have admitted as a rule for these brotherly exchanges, to note both the things which unite us and those which separate us and even place us in opposition to each other.

From the very first lines of your letter, I feel strong fellowship with you in the admiration of those "very ancient authors" to whom you refer: Irenaeus, Tertullian, and St. Cyprian.

It is Irenaeus whom you name first and to whom you refer. You know how deeply venerated he is at Lyons, where he is honored not only as an ecclesiastical writer and a martyr of the Christian Faith but also—and there is a shade of difference—as a Doctor of the Church.

All you say about Irenaeus fills me with joy. You render his thought, which is always our own, with precision and exactitude. We acknowledge in him one of the first witnesses of the authority of the Church in doctrinal matters. However, I would have liked you to go back further still, and to cast a glance on the ecclesiology of St. Ignatius of Antioch, an immediate disciple of the apostles and the second successor to St. Peter as the head of the Church at Antioch. His thought on the subject of the Church, you know, is summarized in one phrase: "Nothing without the bishop." That is to say, and all the epistles of St. Ignatius witness unto this, the rallying point and the center of unity of the Church is the bishop. This means, also, that for him there is in the Church a hierarchy, a teaching, sacramental *authority*, outside of which there is no salvation.

The doctrine of Irenaeus is not different. If he appeals to the unbroken chain of Peter's successors, it is because he is certain—contrary to what Mr. Cullman thinks—that the power of Peter, established by Jesus Christ Himself, has passed to those who have occupied after him, what the centuries from the remotest times have called the *Cathedra Petri*, the Chair of Peter, or the *Sedes Apostolica*, the *Apostolic See*. It is because he considers that the decision emanating from the successors of Peter is of the most sovereign importance due to what he calls by a word which historians have not yet ceased to explain—diversely, anyway—the *potentior principalitas* (the more powerful principality) of the Church of Peter and Paul; that is, the Roman Church.

You give, as regards Irenaeus, a rapid exposition of the Gnostic crisis, which caused the budding Church such danger, to such an extent that, without Jesus Christ, one may well say Christianity would never have come down to us but would have faded in a multiplicity of sects and systems.

I would have liked you to consult, after Irenaeus, St. Cyprian also, whose "ecclesiology," like that of St. Ignatius of Antioch, is centered in the categorical formula: "*Ecclesia in episcopo*—the Church in the bishop" (*Epist.* XXXLLI, 1). This means that for him, just as for all Christian Tradition up to him and down to us Catholics, the Church is a *visible and episcopal society*, an *authoritative society*. So much so that, speaking of the reunion of Churches—a subject dear to our hearts—the English theologian A. Headlam could write in 1920: "The idea of an invisible Church, made popular at the time of the Reformation, is unknown to ecclesiastical antiquity" (Headlam, *The Doctrine of the Church and Christian Reunion*, p. 108).

Undoubtedly, the unity considered by St. Ignatius, St. Irenaeus and then by St. Cyprian, is, above all, that of the local Church, although St. Irenaeus goes beyond that point of view; but, it was necessary that the problem of unity—no longer local, but universal—be faced by us sooner or later.

It is here that I shall beg your permission to stress a few points.

While you were harking back to St. Irenaeus, I was consulting St. Augustine. I was urged to this by the small debate that we had had together about a sentence of Melanchthon, and about the problem of knowing whether it is in St. Augustine that Luther and Calvin could have found their inadmissible doctrine of *absolute predestination*. You return to this in your postscript, and I would like to clarify something here according to the Catholic point of view. You quote an opinion of Msgr. Duchesne. It does not seem to me that that opinion has the sense which you attach to it. Yes, Augustine, after having admitted in the course of his struggle against Manicheism that the free human will could raise itself to the Faith without any divine grace, has, after a more attentive and closer examination of St. Paul, denied that assertion. It is the "Marseillais," following Jean Cassian (that is, those whom, since the seventeenth century we call the Semi-Pelagians), who will take up his doctrine again on this point. However, they were condemned as heretics by the Church at the Council of Orange in A.D. 529. The Council of Trent formulated this decisive canon as the starting point of the Catholic doctrine on justification: "If anyone says that man, by his accomplished works, either by the principles of human nature or by the doctrine of the Law, and without divine grace given by Jesus Christ, can be justified before God, let him be anathema." And also: "If anyone says that, without the preceding inspiration of the Holy Spirit and His help, man can believe, hope, love or repent, as he must in order that the grace of justification be granted to him, let him be anathema."

When Msgr. Duchesne says that Saint Augustine teaches that man can have no *initiative* in the way which leads to salvation, it is this that he means. The *initium fidei* (the beginning of the faith) does not depend on human will alone, but on *prepossessed* liberty aided by grace. But Augustine differs radically from both Luther and Calvin, as we ourselves differ, in that he teaches that free will *cooperates* with grace, that it has the frightful power of rejecting grace, of saying "no" to God, who invites us. Augustine believed in free will. If he had not believed in it, there would have arisen against him, in his time, an irresistible outcry. It suffices to know the history of Pelagianism and Semi-Pelagianism to be convinced of this. So much so, that the following canons of the Council of Trent, directed against Luther and Calvin, could never have been considered as directed against St. Augustine: "If anyone say that the free will of man, put in motion and urged on by God, cooperates in no way with God . . . to prepare itself to obtain the grace of justification; and that it cannot resist grace if it wants to, but that it behaves like an inanimate and inert being, by remaining entirely passive, let him be anathema." "If anyone say that the free will of man, following the sin of Adam, was lost and extinguished, in such a way that it is no longer but a name without reality and even a fiction introduced by Satan into the Church, let him be anathema."

We have no doubt whatever that St. Augustine would have subscribed wholeheartedly to these irrevocable decisions of the Church. He would have done it all the more willingly, even if, accidentally, his intimate sentiments would have been rather divergent—which was not the case—since his ecclesiological doctrine would have made it an obligation which he surely could not have disregarded without contradicting himself.

It is precisely this that I would like to talk about now.

What, then, is the ecclesiology of Augustine? You admit, as I do, the greatness of his genius, the ardent sincerity of his faith, his profound knowledge of the Scriptures, the patient and insinuating charity which he could bring to controversies. We can, therefore, it seems to me, take him as an arbitrator in our discussion about the Church, such as Jesus Christ wished it and founded it. Even if the word "arbitrator" appears too strong to you, it is indisputable that Augustine will be for you, just as for me, an imposing witness of ancient tradition on the subject of the Church.

Now, Augustine has expressed his thought on the Church in three circumstances at least or, more exactly, in the course of the three great controversies which filled his life: the Manichean, the Donatist, and the Pelagian heresies.

The Manicheans constantly invoked reason! This astonishes us in view of the absurdity of their dualism in the course of the ages. Yet "reason" has had other absurdities. The Gnostics also had their logicians, then the Arians and the Semi-Arians. What does Augustine answer? He has a pamphlet on this subject entitled *De Utilitate Credendi* (*On the Usefulness of Believing*). In matters of salvation, he opposes faith to pure reason. And as a manner of imposing faith, he admits that the *Catholica*—as he calls the universal Church —and the *Dei antistites*—that is to say, the bishops—proceed with authority. He approves their action. The family could not subsist, he says, without authority. It is by authority that the child believes that his father is really his father and his mother really his mother. In the same way, society cannot live without authority. Undoubtedly, he says, it would be "shameful to believe in someone without reason." If we believe in Christ, it is because of decisive reasons. For Augustine, there is first the evidence of the peoples converted to Christ and united in the Catholic Church. There is then the *vetustas*, "antiquity," the continuity of the Church, as opposed to heresy, which is always *innovation*. There is, finally and above all, the Gospel, the divine history of Christ, His miracles, the proofs He has given of His divinity. Augustine, in other well-known writings, *De moribus ecclesiae, De catechizandis rudibus, De fide rerum quae non videntur, De vera religione (On Catholic Church Customs, On Instructing the Unlearned, On Faith in Things Unseen, On True Religion)*, never ceases to return to these two points: reason and authority support each other mutually. One does not believe without having considered the reasons for believing. God has deigned to give His reasons: He has manifested Himself throughout the ages by a coherent action of which the Incarnation is the apex, and the Church the beneficiary and the final instrument: God enlightened the Patriarchs. He spoke to Moses and He illumined the Prophets. He finally sent His own Son. His Son, in turn, sent the apostles. Here— a remarkable thing—Augustine applies the word of St. Paul to the Corinthians to Christ Himself (II, 3:2–3): "Our letter, it is you yourselves—a letter written in our hearts— known and read by all men. Yes, it is manifest that you are a letter of Christ written by our care, written not with ink, but with the Spirit of the living God, not on tablets of stone, but on the tablets of flesh which are your hearts."

In the same way, says St. Augustine, Jesus Christ has not written with ink. His letter to the world—His Bible—is the apostles, it is the sovereign authority which He has given them, it is all He has done in His Church and by His Church; that is to say, those miracles, unexplainable without His action and that of the Holy Spirit, the evidences of blood shed by the martyrs, the miracles of purity and charity of the virgins and the widows, the saintliness of the confessors, and also the conquest of peoples.

In his long controversy with the Donatists, Augustine will naturally return to these same ideas. His position in this controversy shows us as well the position which he would adopt in the present problem of the reunion of the Churches. He knew quite well that the Donatists admitted the same dogmas as himself and as the whole Church. What he blamed them for was the fact that they placed themselves outside the unity of the Church. What he wished to obtain from them was their submission to the *Catholica,* filial and total submission. Summarizing his argument, Msgr. Batiffol, in his *Saint Augustin* (I, 269), has written. "The one and universal *Catholica* is such by virtue of a plan of God which the Scripture reveals to us, and through it one will recognize that it is the Church of God. It is necessary to belong to it because, outside of it, there is no salvation. It is holy by its vocation, it is holy in its saints, but it is nonetheless, on earth, *a society in which sinners and saints mingle."*

I underline these last words because I propose to come back to them later, in replying to another part of your letter.

It is especially in the last of these controversies, and in the latter part of his life, while he was in the fullness of his genius and his Scriptural science, that St. Augustine has engraved, so to speak, for the centuries to come, his doctrine on the Church. I would go beyond the limits of a letter if I were to develop it too much. I will therefore limit myself to the famous saying constantly attributed to our great saint: *"Roma locuta est, causa finita est."* In reality, Augustine never pronounced that sentence. Yet one cannot say that the phrase is wrong, because it summarizes his thought very well. It was in the course of a sermon given at Carthage on September 23, 417, during the hottest part of the Anti-Pelagian battle, that Augustine pronounced the following words:

"Two councils have already sent their decisions on this matter to the Apostolic Seat. From there have come the Bulls. *The case is finished*; may the error finally come to an end. That is why we warn them that they take heed; we instruct them that they may be enlightened; we pray that they change."

The Bulls? What does Augustine mean by this word? The term belongs to the judiciary language of the times. The two African councils, which condemned Pelagianism, are able to do nothing decisive, because they did not represent the whole Church. They, therefore, sent their resolutions to the pope —Innocent I—as *relationes* (reports), which they had prepared. The pope, having congratulated them for their deference, answered by *rescripta* (Bulls), that is to say, acts which do not create the law but which interpret it beyond appeal. Augustine recognizes their value so well that he concludes: *"Causa finita est."* The case is finished. There is no coming back to it. The case has been heard.

Why does Augustine attribute so much efficacy to the Bulls of the pope? Solely—and he says it himself—because the pope occupies the *Cathedra Petri*—the Chair of Peter.

Please excuse me, Reverend dear Pastor, for these excessively long developments—too short, though, in view of the seriousness of the subject—concerning the ecclesiological doctrine of St. Augustine.

The sentence I underlined earlier in connection with the mingling of saints and sinners in the Church, leads me to one of the most important parts of your letter.

You assert that "the papacy went through serious moral crises" in the course of the Middle Ages. You add very justly that "the disorders of the Renaissance are notorious."

You conclude that the Church of Leo X could very well no longer be the same as that of Irenaeus. You ask, to say the least, rather disquieting questions about this point: "Have not the ecclesiastical customs and doctrines suffered an evolution which renders the Catholic Church, on certain points, a stranger to the Ancient Church?"

You offer as an example: "Thus we can find in the New Testament neither the prayers for the dead nor the cult of the saints nor the immense role of the Virgin nor pontifical infallibility."

You conclude: "Does this perfect agreement between Scripture and Tradition, which is for Irenaeus the object of no doubt whatever, still exist?"

We are here at the most delicate and, I may say, the most burning point of our friendly discussions.

I would like to be as clear and categorical as possible.

All you say about the moral crises through which the Church has passed during the ages, we admit without any difficulty. We are not afraid of truth in any field whatever. We would blush at a distortion of facts.

Newman has said, somewhere, that Jesus Christ allowed Satan to carry Him, with his arms around His waist, to the pinnacle of the Temple and then to the top of the mountain. Such a thing, Newman says, happened to His Church. When some of the popes were offering the spectacle of a scandalous life, it was Satan who was playing some of his tricks in the heart of the Church herself. Jesus Christ had predicted it in a mysterious word: "Satan has asked to sift you as wheat is sifted!"

We believe that only minds whose faith is weak and badly enlightened can draw from this an objection against the infallibility and indefectibility of the Church. Jesus Christ did not promise that His Church would have only saints. He did not give special privileges in this matter to the hierarchy itself! But he did promise that, *even through sinners*, His own divine authority and that of the Spirit of Truth which He had promised us would pass on.

So, far from constituting an argument against the indefectibility of the Church, one could even maintain that the shortcomings and failings of some of the Roman pontiffs furnish a shining proof of the divine protection with which the Church is surrounded. If it could have died, some of its leaders would have killed it!

Do I exaggerate? Or do you believe that I am expressing here, through a sort of bravado, a personal opinion? Nothing of the sort. I am only repeating the beliefs of a pope, and of a pope who knew by experience what he was talking about. This pope I have quoted in my volume on *The Church at the Time of the Council of Trent*: "Mr. Ambassador," said Pope Paul IV on March 13, 1556, to Navagero, the envoy of Venice to Rome, "for many years this has been in our mind, because we have seen in the house of the Lord many things happening which would have given you scandal . . . It is a miracle, Your Excellency, that this Holy See has been able to maintain itself while our predecessors have done everything to lose it. But it is built on such a rock that it has nothing to fear . . ." (See my book, Vol. XVII, of *The History of the Church*, Fliche et Martin, p. 165).

What is important to notice is that, by a special preservation of the Holy Spirit, not one of the bad popes—and they were few in number, in any case—which history has known, has been accused of having changed anything whatever in the doctrine of the Church. It is in this that the infallibility of the Church suffers no harm through the weaknesses or even the vices of a Borgia, a John XII or a Benedict IX. You have clearly expressed, anyway, that even in those times of moral crises, the Church never lacked very great saints who were working for its restoration, and it is this which I have tried to throw into relief in the volume that I have just quoted above. At the time of Luther and Calvin, outstanding saints were alive. I do not need to name them. They did not touch the doctrine of the Church as Luther and Calvin did. Their saintliness depends very little on these attacks against the Church. I believed I had been able to show that their coming forth was due to the power of life which was inherent in the ancient Church, and thus the Church owes the attackers nothing or almost nothing. Consequently, reserving the name "Revolution" for the "Reformation" of Luther, I rejected the name "Counter-Reformation," bestowed upon the renewal within the Church, since this renewal was itself, not a revolution, but *the only real reformation.* It was then that the magnificent words of our Lord were confirmed—and here I agree with you, Reverend dear Pastor—"And the gates of hell shall not prevail against it."

Before concluding, I would like to thank you also for the words of admiration which you bestow upon St. Gregory the Great, who, no one can doubt, professed the doctrine of *"the Church of authority"* and of the primacy given the successor of Peter over the whole of the *Catholica.*

All you say about him is exact. But this has reminded me of a remark of Luther's taken from *The Table Talk* of Mathesius, for the year 1540: "I would not like to state nor to risk my life on the fact that Jerome and Gregory are among the number of the Blessed, because they taught very badly; one—Jerome—on the question of celibacy; the other —Gregory—on Purgatory and the Sacrifice of the Mass; and yet they are held as being columns of the Church. However, on the subject of Ambrose and Augustine, I have no doubts."

There is another point on which I find difficulty in following you, but where a detailed explanation would lead us too far afield. It is when you list the doctrines of the Catholic Church which, according to you, are not found in the New Testament. You seem in fact to admit that for Irenaeus, and undoubtedly for Cyprian too, for Optatus of Mileve and for Augustine, the perfect agreement between Scripture and Tradition consists in saying "Nothing is found in Tradition which is not found also and beforehand in the New Testament." Such is not our belief. Such was not the faith of Irenaeus, of Cyprian, of Optatus, of Augustine, nor of any of the ancient Fathers. Tradition can never contradict Scripture, but it can very well complete it. It is nowhere stated that Scripture includes everything. It is not through the Scriptures, once again, that Jesus Christ decided to transmit His integral message to us.

This point is so important that I will ask your permission to enlarge upon it before concluding this long letter, the most important, together with yours, in this whole correspondence.

I have already told you once before (and I am sure you agree) that, in order to conduct this debate efficiently, we must put all these important questions *in their context*. We have promised each other to treat vital questions with importance, not to get entangled in details, but to consider truths on an elevated plane and in their continuity.

What, then, is the context here? It consists in this: Jesus Christ was or, rather, is forever the Son of God made man. We believe with all our souls, both you and I, Reverend dear Pastor, in His divinity. Let us, therefore, treat Him as a God—it is the least He can ask of us. Let us not leave Him, so to speak, enclosed within the horizon of His own country and His own age. This is, I fear, what Mr. Cullman does when speaking of the life-time primacy, or even of the temporary primacy of Peter, which is not transmissible to his successors. For Jesus Christ, the Son of God made man, for Jesus Christ, "the Way, the Truth and the Life," there are no limits either in time or in space. He is our Shepherd, for us children of the twentieth century, just as He was that of the Jews of His time. "Everything is bare and uncovered," says the Epistle to the Hebrews, "to the eyes of the One to whom we must render an account." He has, therefore, not provided less for our salvation, us, His lambs of the twentieth century, than He has for the salvation of those lambs of whom He said: "I know my lambs, and my lambs know me; I call them by their names . . ." He is calling us by our names, Reverend dear Pastor, you as well as me. I affirm, therefore, that He could not have abandoned us, that He had foreseen for us means of certitude in the Faith, and that these means cannot be different from what they were during the first centuries, to wit: one Church, the depositary of one Scripture and Tradition, commissioned to transmit His message, unalloyed with error, till the end of time.

That our present preoccupations with free examination or individual Biblicism, without the control of a superior and definite authority, is totally foreign to the thought of Christ —that is what seems to me to stand out in the pages of the Gospel. Before Jesus Christ, certainly, the Doctors of the Law had full freedom. They opposed one school to the other, Hillel to Schammai, Sadducees to Pharisees. But as soon as Jesus Christ started speaking, as soon as He opened His mouth, the less understanding ones noticed something totally new, something strange which filled the Masters of the Law with astonishment, then jealousy and finally a deicide-hatred. What, then, was the manner of speaking of Christ?

St. Mark said it extremely well, in his first chapter: "We were astonished at his teaching, because he taught *as one who had authority* and not as the Scribes." And a little later, after He had chased out a devil, the Evangelist adds: "All were astonished, to the point of wondering amongst themselves: 'What is this? A teaching given *with authority*! . . .'" (Mark 1:22, 27).

Now, Jesus Christ never changed His style nor His tone. He always spoke *with authority*. He ordered His apostles to speak in their turn with authority, and He declared: "As the Father hath sent me, so I send you!" And also: "Whoever listens to you, listens to me; and whoever listens to me, listens to him who sent me." St. Paul always spoke with authority. The other apostles did the same. That Jesus Christ had foreseen for His Church a long career throughout the centuries—that is clear from His words: "Behold, I shall be with you till the end of time!" Or also: "The gates of hell shall not prevail against it!"

He was, then, not God, if one supposes that He ignored the long task imposed upon His Church in the midst of men, until the Gospel shall have been preached to all peoples! This would be, in our eyes, an unbearable blasphemy! That he should have left redeeming truth to the infinite discussions of men, or that he should have accepted "yes" or "no" beforehand, on the most important subjects—the seven sacraments, the Real Presence in the Eucharist, the sacrificial oblation in the Mass, the cult due to His saints associated to the one which we offer to Him, the notion of hell, and so on—it is this that we cannot believe, because it would not be worthy of a God. If the Church misleads us—an unthinkable thing for us—it is He who misleads us! Never will we stoop so low as to believe that!

It seems to me that these few reflections lead us straight to the examination of ecumenism, which we have already spoken of several times in our letters and about which we must, it seems to me, debate. Be sure, Reverend dear Pastor, that I shall always do it in the same spirit of brotherhood and Christian charity, even if we are ultimately unable to identify our points of view. I do not believe in the efficacy of dialectics in such matters. I would rather put myself for the present and the future in the hands of divine grace, which we shall both implore of common accord.

Please accept, Reverend and dear Pastor, my respectful sentiments in our Lord.

L. CRISTIANI

X

† / †

"The Remission of Sins"

19.

Dear Canon Cristiani,

After the consideration of the Church, the *Credo* leads us to forgiveness of sins: "I believe in the remission of sins." This brief declaration, pertinent to all of us, is especially salutary at the end of this brotherly discussion, where, more than anywhere else, our finger touches the tragedy of our separation. It is rare in the case of divorce that each party does not have its share of wrongs. As Protestants, we certainly had ours: mockery, scorn, sometimes hatred, and violence in reply to violence; often we were satisfied with not being Catholics instead of striving to become Christians. One of my parishioners made this judicious remark yesterday: "We do not do enough of those things of which Catholics do too much." Coming from a simple man, it describes very aptly an aspect of our spiritual situation. It happens that because of our reaction against authority, we confuse laziness with liberty! Now, real liberty is found in submission to

Christ, and not in a desire not to resemble those from whom we have separated ourselves.

Forgiveness of sins is the supreme gift of the Saviour to the believer. The repetition of the Our Father's petition "Forgive us our trespasses as we forgive those who trespass against us," the candid evening prayer where we implore God to wipe away our faults of the fading day, the religious practice of placing ourselves before the holiness of the Omnipotent One who is outraged by our misdeeds, are so many opportunities to ask for and to receive absolution. You have certainly heard recited the beautiful prayer which Theodore of Beze composed: "Lord God, Father everlasting and omnipotent, we recognize and we confess before Thy holy majesty that we are poor sinners, born in corruption, inclined towards evil, incapable of ourselves of doing good, who transgress every day and in various ways Thy holy precepts . . ."

This opening part which describes our wretchedness corresponds to the *Confiteor* of the Mass. In the Calvinistic rite, the confession of sins comes immediately after the reading of the summary of the Law. The officiating minister rereads the double rule: "Thou shalt love the Lord thy God with thy whole heart . . . Thou shalt love thy neighbor as thyself."

The conscience of the faithful causes his anger, his wickedness, his infidelities to pass in review before him. He is, if he truly participates in the divine service, overwhelmed by the realization of his faults. How many times have I, for my part, bowed down my head before the implacable exactitude of the words which I use: "Poor, poor human nature," I used to think, "with the miserable thoughts which passed through our heads, such as meanness and jealousy! How far are we from Thy will, O Lord Jesus!" The past, also, swirls round in my head: obstinate adolescence, intellectual pride of my youth, and ingratitude. Confession over, how sweet it is to repeat for one's companions and for oneself one of the beautiful verses culled from the liturgy: "Even if your sins should be as scarlet, they will become white as snow"; or with the Lord Himself: "God so loved the world that he gave his only Son in order that whoever believes in him, will not perish, but will have life everlasting"; or still more simply: "My child, thy sins are forgiven thee."

Whoever is impressed with theology may certainly find predestined determinism in the expression "incapable of doing good of ourselves"; or the Lutheran disputation against the merit of good works in the use of the text (Eph. 2:8): "It is by grace that you are saved, by means of faith. And that does not come from you. It is the gift of God." The knowledge of particular doctrines figures little in the soul of the immense majority; there exists the gravity of my sins and the goodness of God which wipes them away. For the rest —the discussion of specialists disappears before the spiritual reality itself.

I have already spoken about the sacraments and the part they play in our piety. Whether it is a question of the Lord's Supper, of baptism or, as here, of the simple Sunday worship, forgiveness is at the center of our faith. Pardon is the gift of God. The liberating words are given because of His coming among us, because of His suffering, death, and resurrection. He is forgiveness. He is "the Lamb of God, who takes away the sins of the world." He annihilates the original curse; the gate, closed for so long a time, opens up before the awestruck soul. Hope is born out of the consideration of the work accomplished for mankind. Forgiveness, which changes our relationship with God, also transforms human relations. A law different from that of the jungle and the claw descends on earth through the channel of mercy.

On the occasion of each marriage, while presenting to the newly-weds the Bible, which inserts the message of God into their home, I draw attention to the unique role of Jesus

Christ in the union of their two hearts. Only He communicates confidence in the Father, who dispenses daily Life, and with it, according to our needs, sometimes joy, sometimes sorrow. Only He teaches true love, which makes us carry the burden of the other and makes us forget ourselves. He, alone, in a word, places the spirit of tolerance in my heart. He teaches me to discover in my life-companion that limitation which is inherent in human nature, and which He has shown exists in myself. I must love as I have been loved; pardon as I have been pardoned. Without pardon, the most exalted ideal changes quickly into a vengeful justice, a source of innumerable conflicts. What is applicable to the family is applicable to other earthly relationships: the factory, the office, government and the Church.

You will allow me to be brief regarding the last two affirmations of the *Credo*. I have already spoken about the Resurrection in connection with Christ ascending into heaven. It is the corollary to a pardon which redeems the whole man: the *spirit, soul and body* (I Thess. 5:23). Perhaps it is not useless to underline that the word "flesh" is interpreted generally in the Reformed Churches with relation to the reflections of St. Paul: "What is sown in corruption rises in incorruption; what is sown in dishonor rises in glory; what is sown in weakness rises in power; what is sown a natural body rises a spiritual body" (I Cor. 15:42–43). We distinguish "flesh" from what the word "carnal" represents in current language; the flesh becomes a synonym for the body; and I have a few colleagues who, to avoid confusion, speak of "the resurrection of the bodies." Indeed, it is I who will arise, but transformed by the power of God, in whom all is possible and for whom the resurrection is equivalent to a new creation. Because of this persuasion cremation has spread more and more among us; and in a city such as where I am writing, it is a rare occasion to take part in a burial.

Finally, the last phrase of the *Credo* is "life everlasting." It forecasts the definitive return to our paternal home after the long pilgrimage on earth, the goal in the unchangeable light of God, far from darkness and far from sin, for, the Apocalypse sings, "The first things will have disappeared; mortality, grief and pain will vanish like the fog with the rising sun."

Let us make the point, if you indeed wish it. I see no essential difference between a Protestant and a Catholic, neither about the Author of all things, who is God, nor about the Author of salvation, who is Christ, nor about the principle of the Holy Spirit working among us, nor about the end which is, through the pardon of sin and the Resurrection, life everlasting. Secular discussions revolve about what it is convenient to call "the means of grace." The Protestant in practice converses directly with God the Father, Son and Holy Spirit. Submissive to the Decalogue, he ignores the Commandments of the Church, whereas Catholicism insists on the importance of the intermediaries: to wit, the Virgin, the saints, the priest on the spiritual plane, the hierarchy on the intellectual and disciplinary plane. If our correspondence would examine systematically all points of differences, it ought to tackle several other questions. Let us limit ourselves to the main ones: Protestantism repudiates the veneration of saints, the cult of images, along with the Commandments of the Church, the prescription of fasting, the obligation of confessing to a priest, the forbidding of mixed marriages. Assistance at divine worship is a moral obligation, and Communion, while enthusiastically recommended, is never obligatory. Finally, it would be necessary to devote an entire study to the role of the laity in the direction of the Church. Generally, they are the majority in the councils and synods, with the result that the pastors do not guide the bark. Their advice certainly carries great weight, but the Church does not belong to them.

I have, of course, made only a sketch, and you will correct what is excessive in my simplification; yet it was easy, because it retained at least an aspect of our century-old secular quarrel. As I meditate on this problem, I often wonder whether our two Churches are not two opposite teaching bodies, as well as two doctrinal systems. One offers staffs of support, guardians. The other lets the trees grow in the wind under the safekeeping of the sun alone. The first is more gentle but restrains liberty; the second is bolder and demands more of an individual, but grants him, in obedience to Jesus Christ, a considerable margin of responsibility and, consequently, of independence. Protestantism does not spare us either contests or gropings. As Canon Moreton (*Rome and the Primitive Church*, p. 14) remarks: "It does not seem to me that our Lord sought to spare men every individual effort. On the contrary, He encourages them to reflect always, and to study all problems personally."

It suffices to reread our two important letters on the Church to see how our concepts are clearly opposite. However, both of us believe in the holy, universal Church. You attribute to the hierarchy an infallibility which I contest. Whoever will read our correspondence, will weigh, in the light of our expositions, the *pro* and the *con*. The debate is held at one and the same time on the spiritual and on the intellectual plane. Does there exist a third neutral plane which can separate us? I doubt it. You have the living experience of Catholicism, which I am not aware of; and I, that of Protestantism, to which you are a stranger. With both of us, attachment of the heart mingles with our reason. Our examination is free, surely, but our leanings play their role in our decisions. "I do not believe in the efficacy of dialectics in such a matter," you wrote to me. What precedes is very close to that judgment. Yet the effort at objectivity and search for truth to which we two have devoted ourselves has its value. It permits—when it could be only that—the clear definition of the main question of separation. As regards Augustine—this will be the only completion to your last letter which I shall add—I must make it clear that his authority for us is not equivalent to that of Scripture. We appreciate his keen sense of our misery far from God, and his stirring joy before the grace which snatches him from the depths, but we remain astonished and even scandalized by his attitude towards the Donatists. How could a man who believed equally in the irresistible call of God and in free will—allow me this paradox which bears the marks of our debate—have maintained the thesis of compelling them to enter the Church, and that on a text arbitrarily taken from St. Luke (14:23)? For him (Letter 185) force is an arm which the Catholic princes might use to bring their subjects to the Faith whether by fines, exile or confiscation. Did not Tertullian give this warning: "It is not the duty of religion to force religion"? And our Lord before him (Luke 9:55)? Augustine, like Calvin, seems to us to be a fallible disciple, above whom, as above all Christians, we place Christ, the only perfect being, alone God (Matt. 23:8–12), and the unshakeable foundation of Peter and of the whole Church, wherever it be on earth.

For four centuries one has seen Protestants pass over to Catholicism, and *vice versa.* Yet no sensible displacement of numbers has resulted. You have your convictions, and I mine. We are neither of us twenty years old. We have carried on this correspondence more with the sincere desire of explaining ourselves, than with the hope of convincing each other. Under these conditions, could we have perceived more than a *modus vivendi,* a way of living, between us? Does the birth of an ecumenical movement in the twentieth century seriously modify the views of the future? Will we soon go beyond that stage of tolerance which in France and Switzerland is replacing the contests of yesterday to advantage? That is the question which I shall examine in my next letter, if you indeed wish it.

Kindly accept in the meanwhile, Reverend dear Canon, the expression of my faithful esteem in our Lord.

JEAN RILLIET

20.

Reverend and dear Pastor,

Like you, I must enter upon the very important question of the remission of sins, such as it is understood and practiced in the Catholic Church. As you well said in the course of your letter, "Secular discussions revolve about what it is convenient to call 'the means of grace.'" We believe, as you, that the "Author of all things is God," that the "Author of salvation is Christ," and that this end, life everlasting, is secured "by pardon of our sins and the Resurrection."

Assuredly, like you, we attach great value to these words of the Our Father: "Forgive us our trespasses as we forgive those who have trespassed against us," and our theologians teach that this invocation, made from the bottom of the heart, suffices to wipe out what we may call "daily sins," that dust of small omissions that we are surely obliged to acknowledge in our daily life.

In the same context I shall speak of general liturgical confession, which is made by us at the beginning of each Mass at the foot of the altar. However, we go much further than that in the exercise of "the power of the keys," as the power to remit sin is called among us.

The power to remit sins is effected in a *sacrament,* a second plank of salvation after baptism, a sort of supplement to baptism, which can be bestowed only once but whose promises are not, alas! always kept by the Christian. What to do about those sins committed after baptism? This is, nevertheless, the most normal situation among Christians of today, who are all, or practically all, baptized from their birth. What to do about those sins which are not always venial, those which can be and often are "mortal sins," that is, those which cause the loss of grace and divine friendship in the soul?

The Protestant solution, if I understand it well, is to link the remission of sins, even the most serious, to that general and impersonal confession which is made in the liturgical gatherings of our two worships.

We Catholics do not believe that one can stop there, or that the pardon of grievous faults can be obtained so cheaply. Without doubt, we are exceedingly less severe in this matter than were the first Christians, who excluded from the Christian communion those who were guilty of certain notably heinous faults, such as apostasy, murder and adultery. We condemn the rigorism of Tertullian, who reproved Pope Callistus I for his excessive leniency in remitting sins. We no longer make persons, guilty of big crimes or grave faults, hidden or public, perform public penances, or even very long private penances. The period of "listed penances" is gone beyond recall. They were applications of the principles of the remission of sin which the times exacted, perhaps, but which the discipline of the Church has the right to soften. We have even evolved a great deal since Jansenism, whose severity turned so many souls from Christian practice by discouraging them and by not taking sufficient account of human weaknesses.

Despite all these alleviations, which I regard as having been necessary and beneficial, we do not believe that Protestantism was right in abolishing the sacrament of Penance, insofar as it is a sacrament, and to refuse to the representatives of Jesus Christ the right to exercise the power conferred on them for the good of souls.

Let us approach the problem directly.

In the sacrament of Penance there are three acts to be accomplished on the part of the penitent, without which he cannot obtain pardon: contrition, confession, and satisfaction. I believe that we would easily agree about contrition and satisfaction. But it is confession which creates the difficulty.

To bring out into the clear the origin of confession is our business. That it is the invention of men is difficult to admit. It is unpleasant for us all. Do not think that it is for his own pleasure that a confessor closes himself in a tight and uncomfortable box called the confessional, to hear there the monotonous and pitiable review of the weaknesses of the soul and the flesh, often through hours and even whole days. No! If we were not face to face with a divine institution, it would be to our advantage, especially in these times of the shortage of priests, to renounce this kind of ministry. Yet we have no right to do so. We would betray our mission if we withdrew before what—in a brutal word, a common word, a vulgar word even, but an exact one—we would have to call "drudgery."

Let us ask the Curé of Ars (whose astonishing life you have perhaps read, so infused with the supernatural) why, during thirty years of his life, he kept to the confessional in his small church at Ars; why he lent his ear, on an average of fourteen to sixteen hours a day, to the confessions of pilgrims who came running from all parts of France, and often even from foreign lands! Despite the appalling weariness that his ministry imposed on him, he would answer us, unquestionably, with the remark which authentically comes from himself: "One will know only at the Last Judgment the good that is done in the confessional."

We are not all of us saints. Far from it! And we groan because of it. We are not all Curés of Ars, but I believe that collectively we would adopt his remark by generalizing it: "One will not know except at the Last Judgment all the good that was done through the centuries in our confessionals; one will know only then the number of guilty souls who have found therein peace and happiness; one will see only then the immensity of the river of grace which has flowed from the Catholic confessional."

This indisputable benefit would already be an argument, a very strong one for confession. However, it is not the principal one. What is more important for us to know is what Jesus Christ wanted.

From one end of our debate to the other, Reverend dear Pastor, we need not seek anything else. Personal relationships, human practices, and local or general customs have no weight here except in the measure in which we can link them incontestably to the will and the effective institution of Christ.

Without doubt, from the moment when we have admitted and, according to us, proved that Jesus Christ entrusted the message that He brought to the world to a living, infallible and indefectible Church, the question is completely settled by the teaching and secular practice of the Church. Here we have, in addition, for those who wish at any price, and not unreasonably, to find a text or scriptural texts in support of the theses which we examine, some categoric declarations of our Gospels. The Council of Trent had recourse on this point to two principal texts: "Whatever you shall bind on earth shall be bound also in heaven; and what you shall loose on earth shall likewise be loosed in heaven" (Matt. 18:18); and "sins shall be remitted to those to whom you shall remit them, and shall be retained for those for whom you shall retain them" (John 20:23). The first of these texts is very general. It is applied not only to sins, but to all kinds of bonds which can be imposed on our consciences, to disciplinary laws notably. But it is limitless and is evidently applicable to the most serious bonds of all—those of sin. The Church in her hierarchy has received the power *to bind* and *to loose*. In the second text it is specifically a question rather of the power to remit or retain sin. However, a sin is by definition something intimate, personal, hidden from the eyes of men. It is not what one sees in the sin—and one does not see all—which counts, but the bad intention, the internal perversity, the rebellion against the law of God and the order of conscience.

It is exactly the essentially hidden character of sin which creates the obligation of avowal; that is, of confession. The priest, as depositary of the power conferred by Jesus Christ, cannot retain or remit lightly; he must know what he is doing; he acts in the name of God Himself. He is a judge in His court. The first obligation of a judge is to examine the case before pronouncing judgment. Here, however, the instruction concerns entirely the confession of the sinner. It is all the more evident since there is no question here of the materiality of the deeds in accusation, but of the new attitude of the penitent towards his faults. Suppose a sinner should come to the confessional to make a frank and complete avowal of his sins, even the most horrible, but without any feeling of repentance, without any desire to redeem himself. He could not, of course, receive absolution. God does not pardon without repentance. What makes the eternity of the punishment of hell, according to us, is the eternity of sin, the will never to bow down, never to submit, never to recognize the supreme dominion of God.

In order that the remission of sin take place in the court of penance, in order that the sinner be assured of pardon, in order that peace return to his soul, in order that his heart may repeat ecstatically the words of Christ: "He who has received the greater pardon is he who loves more"—an utterance which a Pharisee cannot understand, but which a Mary Magdalen will clearly understand—for all these reasons, I say, there is need of confession which is founded on humility, regret, frankness, loyalty, hope and confidence.

This is not the place to give a history of confession throughout the ages. In this matter, there has taken place an evolution, as there is evolution in all that lives. The oak of five hundred years scarcely resembles the kernel from which it emerged. The evolution of life is, thus, legitimate and providential.

I shall speak no more about sacramental confession. It is evidently one of the major points of difference between us. At least, grant us the justice of thinking that, if we hold on to it so tenaciously even to the point where nothing shall ever be able to make us renounce it, we do so, not for any human motive or any human interest, but solely in the absolute conviction that Jesus Christ bestowed it on us as an immense power for the greatest good of souls. Truly, these souls find not only pardon in the confession (a thing which would already be wonderful), but enlightment, advice, counsels, encouragement, a whole "spiritual medication," with the result that the priest confessor is not only a judge, but also a director, a friend and, if one dare say it, a "psychiatrist," whose cures, entirely spiritual, are most of the time more effective and salutary than the interventions of the doctors of the body.

I have enlarged at length on all this, and I would not like to prolong this letter beyond bounds. There remains just enough space to touch on two points:

Firstly, you tell me that the practice of cremation is tending to spread around you. That surprises me, and I did not believe it up to now. With us, on the contrary, the practice of cremation is formally forbidden by Canon Law. It jars against I know not what feeling of respect towards the mortal remains of the Christian. I recognize that no truth of dogmatic regulation is at stake here, but the prescriptions of Canon Law seem worthy of respect to us, and we should not willingly treat them lightly.

Secondly, in your recapitulation, you set forth that the Protestant addresses himself directly to God without an intermediary, whereas we pass through the Church. I would like to make a timely clarification here. The Church for me, for us, is not a strange power; it is ourselves, it is I, it is the whole mystical body of Christ. Thus, I address myself directly to God, to Jesus, as to a Friend, as to a Brother, as to my Spouse. I cannot feel more separated from Him than you. In the instances of elevated prayer, or in the fervor of Eucharistic Communion, I love, and we all love to repeat the sublime words of St. Paul: "I live no more, but it is Jesus who lives in me!" Or again, "My beloved is mine, and I am His." Catholic piety is, then, collective, not individual; or rather it is individual as well as collective. I do not know whether I make myself clear. When I take my breviary, when I go up the altar to celebrate Mass, when a Catholic enters a Church to pray, or prays in the secret of his own dwelling, he must know that the whole Church is in him and with him, that he represents her. I say my breviary in the name of the Church; I celebrate my Mass in the name of the Church. Everything I do for God is of profit for the whole Christian community. It is that very thing which is contained in this phrase of the *Credo* which you recite as we do: "I believe in the communion of saints." The Church, then, is not a different authority on whom I have always fixed an oblique glance to know whether she approves or disapproves of me! No, we form a single unity! In the same way that the soul is wholly in the whole body and wholly in each part of the body, so the Church is wholly in all Catholicity and wholly in each Catholic! That whole Church in me is united directly with her God, with her Jesus!

Kindly accept, my dear Pastor, the respect of my very devoted sentiments in our Lord.

L. CRISTIANI

XI

† / †

Ecumenism

21.

Dear Canon Cristiani,

After the crumbling away which characterizes the nineteenth century for Protestants, they have been reacting energetically for fifty years against the exaggerated individualism to which they had momentarily paid sacrifice. Consequently a hundred years ago, for example, when the question arose about union with the State, and free Churches formed together, which, no longer desiring any official subsidy, built their own chapels and paid their own clergy, our age has been assisting at a series of reunions. The Reformed Church of Scotland, that of Neuchatel in Switzerland and, nearer to us, the Reformed Church of France have reestablished themselves in their ancient unity. The motives of division had lost their sharpness, and an evolution had taken place on the part of one and the others; the cause of the schism suddenly appeared inconsequential, and an agreement was reached, not without—let us underline it in passing—mutual concessions.

On the international plan the impetus for reunion sprang

from the missionary societies. In the same countries, converted pagans see the work of clerics of various denominations and are astonished that the representatives of Jesus Christ all wave a different flag. Following the universal Missionary Conference in 1910, the Anglican Bishop Brent decided to go back to the root of the evil. He won over to his viewpoint several influential men, and ended on the eve of the First World War with the foundation of the Universal League for International Friendship by means of the Churches. Under the aegis of the Swedish Archbishop Soederblom, the movement was enlarged and became ecumenism with its two branches: Life and Work, and Faith and Order. I have already mentioned in a previous letter the amazement and joy which shook Christianity when, for the first time, Archimandrites, Anglican and Swedish bishops, Presbyterian clergymen, Lutheran and Calvinistic pastors participated in the same worship. Since then, the practice has spread in many of our cities whereby in common manifestations readings, prayers and speeches were apportioned to a priest of the Greek Church, an Anglican chaplain, and an Old Catholic *curé*. This manifestation of unity is sometimes a little theatrical—solemn processions where sacerdotal vestments of different rites mix—yet it does not affect any the less those who return through it to the words of Saint Paul in his letter to the Ephesians (4:45): "There is only one body, and one Spirit alone, there is only one baptism, one God alone, and Father of all, who is above all, and among us and in us."

For my part, I have always deeply regretted the refusal of Catholicism to join these manifestations, and that for one reason in particular: the non-Protestant Christian whom I keep in touch with continuously in this country is neither Anglican nor Lutheran nor Orthodox, but Catholic. Our churches are very near. Often the faithful Protestants who are making their way to church cross the path of the

zealous Catholic who is on his way to Mass. We are a mixed
country, I have told you. Our trades make us work side by
side. Marriages are born continually out of this proximity,
and if, little by little, confessional peace is established, the
occasion when a family in formation decides to ask for the
help of the pastor or of the priest becomes a source of cruel
difficulties. Why should not the contact established with the
Orthodox which permits us to go back beyond the time of
Leo IX and Michael Cerularius inspire you? The permissions
granted by the *Monitum* of the Holy Office of February 28,
1950, authorizes certain private meetings, but these permissions are accompanied by so many reservations that they lose
the greatest part of their value. The bridges erected during
and after the war between one confession and another
should, on the contrary, be multiplied and enlarged. For its
modest role, our correspondence is one of them. May God
grant that one day we may celebrate a *Te Deum* in common,
in one of your holy sanctuaries, and, to avoid any idea of
annexation, repeat it according to our rites in one of our
churches, St. Peter's at Geneva or the Cathedral of Lausanne.

But the dream sweeps me away! Let us return to reality.
M. Gabriel Marcel has underlined this unity in a remarkable chapter of *Christian Unity and Religious Tolerance*; it
is not a coalition of different forces, but the certitude of a
common belongingness: "We are one since we are sons of
the same Father." And I shall add "ransomed by the same
Saviour." Division derives from a fault committed either by
some or by others or by both at the same time. It casts over
the Gospel, the common treasure of all Christian confessions,
a funereal veil. You have seen the role played in the genesis
of ecumenism by the missionary problem. In the face of the
impious forces of this age our rival clock bells are also a
scandal.

How can this conflict which opposes unity and truth be

resolved? If we are equally convinced of the justice of our positions, on the important points at least, capitulation is impossible. I cannot through love of unity pass over one objection, one doubt. The only attitude permissible seems to me to be the act of waiting, with eyes wide open and searching, and with the constant willingness to reconsider my faith, waiting in study, prayer and charity. Submission demands conviction, failing which it quickly deteriorates into hyprocrisy. To don the uniform of a friendly group in order to attach myself to it without intellectual conquest is to risk a horrible awakening one day.

Fidelity to received truth easily leads to scorn for the holders of a different persuasion. Then it is necessary to beg from God the grace of a large and trusting heart. Good will comes from on high. While our Lord was being questioned by the Samaritan woman on the respective merits of the temple of Sychar and that of Jerusalem, He made this astonishing reply: "Believe me, the hour is coming when you will adore the Father neither on this mountain nor in Jerusalem. The hour is coming, and is already come when the true adorers will adore the Father in spirit and truth; for they are the adorers whom the Father asks for" (John 4:21). The remark "the hour is already come" is born of a loving clarification capable of piercing partitions and of making known hearts, wherever they are found, which bow down before God. We must note that Christ accords a supremacy of the Jews over the Samaritans: "You adore," He specifies, "what you do not know, but we adore what we know, for salvation comes from the Jews" (v. 22). If, however, He distinguishes a true tradition from a false one, truth in its bareness is not sufficient! The Spirit must be added to it. Is it rash to think, on considering this text, that sometimes the Spirit uses incomplete doctrines, narrow luminous rays to attach a soul to Himself? You raised the question of *Catholicism in intention* in a preceding letter, by inscribing in the soul of your Church a man who is a stranger to it exteriorly. I replied that we consider a Catholic who is penetrated by the spirit of Jesus Christ to be a true Christian. Does not this identical reaction, despite the difference of words, indicate the form of unity which can provisionally bind together visibly separated brothers? Do not baptism, the Father, the Son and the Holy Spirit weigh heavier on the scales than symbolism and transubstantiation, or ecclesiastical republicanism or the hierarchy, or a lowly or glorious concept of the saints? This can be said without falling into relativism.

In the light of ecumenical experience, I must proceed further and try to examine the future. What has permitted Stockholm, Lausanne, Oxford, Edinburgh and Amsterdam, and what will make Evanston worth something, is the admission of a gathering on a footing of complete equality. Orthodox, Anglicans and Protestants have extended their hands without order of precedence. They have not established the categories of the past. The Churches of the sixteenth century, those of the seventeenth and the eighteenth —Presbyterian or Methodist—sit down side by side with the representatives of Orthodoxy. The presidency of the plenary sessions of Amsterdam was successively entrusted to Pastor Boegner, to the Anglican Archbishop of Canterbury, to the Swedish Archbishop of Uppsala, to the Orthodox Archbishop of Thyatire, to Dr. John Nott, to Dr. Henry Van Dusen and to Bishop Bromley Oxnam. After great social upheavals, it is an accepted principle that foreign governments will recognize the new government of an overthrown people. Ought not the "children of the light" to possess in this matter the "intelligence of the children of the world," too? Ecumenism, which reaches out a hand to Catholicism, seems to me to demand a gesture which is surely hard for it.

Anglicans and Swedes play a very important role in these huge conventions. Their hybrid situation explains it: at the moment of the Reformation, a great part of the episcopacy, whether in Sweden or in England, rallied to the proposed changes. As a consequence, the transformation of the Church was less radical; the cathedrals passed to the new regime with arms and baggage. Titles, crosses, mitres, altars perpetuated themselves in a worship penetrated by Protestantism. Bishops in their old age consecrated new bishops, but, by a concurrence of circumstances which I believe providential, the first ceremonies were tarnished with irregularity. Ours is not to argue here once again the famous debates which ended in 1896 with the condemnation of Anglican Orders by Leo XIII. Viewed from a Catholic angle, the Anglican episcopacy is illegitimate, the Swedish one more so; viewed by the Churches of England and Sweden, it is bound directly with the Middle Ages and antiquity. The subsistent incertitude facilitates the relationships with the non-ordained which we are, while the legitimacy postulated permits contact with the Oriental rites. After the decision of 1896, I do not see how Protestantism, deprived of the titles of belief other than Baptism, could hope from you a hand officially extended in equality. However, we must come to that point!

You see the route of organic unity bristles with obstacles apparently insurmountable. They have spoken in your circles of a "return." Such a view is illusionary. They can hope for the surrender of a small group of isolated rebels through indifference. The large Churches, the fragments of Christianity which are sufficient unto themselves, will not deny their past. They consider themselves to be the Church of Christ, just as Mr. Coty would believe himself to be France in the face of the Bourbons restored to the throne of Spain! Unless we care to look at this aspect of reality frankly, we should be laboring under the danger of nourishing illusions. As long as the Vatican will not truly welcome us as brothers, unity will be isolated to the merely spiritual. There will remain personal esteem, and trust which binds a pastor to a priest, a follower of the Mass to a follower of the Pulpit—

which is, at one and the same time, little and much. You spoke in your first letter of "a necessary and divine intransigence." Be sure that this will be reciprocal, apart from equality.

I should like to speak in a different tone. Frankness and a lucid examination of our respective positions forbid me. That is why, on the plane of officialdom, like Sister Anne on the tower of Bluebeard, I still see nothing coming. Within the perspective of ecclesiastical absolutism, the dusty and sun-burnt way remains deserted. However, my respect for you and the confidence which permits you to write to me, protest. God will trace out new ways, I am convinced. He alone knows by what preliminary upheavals He will cause our secular edifice to pass away.

Setting my face to the future, will it be permitted me to formulate a twofold desire? Firstly, there is a term which I would like to see erased from ecclesiastical vocabulary, except for rare cases: that of "heretics." It is not asking little. The word "heresy" goes back to the origin of the Church. It is found in the Epistles of Paul and in the Acts of the Apostles. Among the Jews, it designated a tendency of piety—the *"airesis"* of the Pharisees and the Sadducees (Acts 5:17, 15:5, 26:5). The Jews applied it later to Christianity and qualified Paul as the head of the "Nazarene *airesis*." Paul used it twice: in connection with the divisions at the time of the Communion of the Corinthians, where certain ones made a band apart and banqueted gluttonously while their companions went hungry (I Cor. 11:9). The separation in that case was witness to pride and contempt. The separated ones wished their table and their own special form of food. The word strikes at a parochial attitude, not an aberration of intellect. It is found again in Galatians (5:20) with the same signification, in the enumeration of the works of the flesh. One has to wait for the Epistle to Titus (3:10) and the Second Epistle of Peter (2:1) to meet this term being applied to growing

Gnosticism, to those men who desert good works in order to lead themselves into foolish discussions and absurd genealogies. When one realizes through the reading of Irenaeus the immanentism of the Valentiani and other sectaries, one sees to what extent such systems imply rejection of Christ. Peter is more explicit: *"Heretics deny the Master who redeemed us."* Do we not find in these words of the Apostle the only definition of heresy which carries weight for the Christian? In the light cast on this problem by the chief apostle of the Church, a Protestant and an Anglican refuse absolutely to be ranged alongside of that motley crowd of heretics. "Where Christ is, there is the Church" is a certain saying of our theologians. Christians, such as we are, merit perhaps censures but certainly not that. Between the style of the Middle Ages and that of our day a noticeable evolution has taken place which ought definitely to have repercussions in Canon Law and the manuals of history. A separated brother is not a heretic in the sense of Peter 2:1.

My second desire is a complete and universal admission on the part of Rome of liberty of conscience and worship. It is beyond me to exaggerate the discomfiture which reigns among my co-religionists today, who are most desirous to come to an agreement, when they notice that the Vatican seems to operate on two levels and to claim for Catholic minorities the rights which they refuse to Protestants in Spain and in Colombia. We can justifiably attribute to it enough influence to make her voice heard in Madrid and Bogotá. Recent concordats give our faithful in those countries the position of outcasts. Official documents exist, signed by the governments of Catholic countries and by Rome. What, then, does she desire? I shall not go back to the unfortunate *Syllabus*, more than eighty years old. More recent documents leave us dreaming; for example, we find in the encyclical *Non abbiamo bisogno* of Pius XI the subtle distinction—too subtle—between "the 'liberty of consciences,' the rights which souls have to gain the greatest spiritual good under the magistracy and educative work of the Church," and "the 'liberty of conscience,' a *dubious* expression used to signify the absolute independence of conscience, an absurd thing in a soul created and redeemed by God." (These texts are drawn from the *Human Community according to the Christian Spirit*, gathered from pontifical documents, Fribourg, 1944, pp. 99–100.) Such reflections are mirrored in those of Leo XII in *Libertas praestantissimum, On the Liberty of Worship and Freedom of Conscience*. I shudder particularly before the fearsome remark: "It is in no wise permitted to ask, defend or accord, without discernment, liberty of thought, of the press, of teaching, of religions, as so many rights that nature has conferred on man," and the corrective: "It follows likewise that these different kinds of liberties can, for just causes, be tolerated." (*Op. cit.*, p. 30, also pp. 21–29.) Do those in high place take account of the trouble cast in our souls by such reservations? How is it, we think indignantly, that we open wide the gates of our cities —and they thank us for it—that we let them build cathedrals and schools on our soil, and yet they would refuse this same privilege to ours in the land of Franco and in such a South American country! Cannot the situation of the Protestants in France serve as a model? Does not French Catholicism, far from suffering from the full liberty granted to us since Napoleon, march on intellectually and spiritually at the head of Catholic nations, decidedly, very decidedly in advance of Spain and Colombia?

Was it better to remain silent on these reflections? Our correspondence would have carried the weight of that silence. If the glance cast on the future reveals the force which the testimony of a united Christianity would acquire, it also points out the gestures without which the cause of unity will proceed only under difficulty. Meetings are usually held half-way between two points of division.

Since I have hazarded these desires, which are almost advice, I shall devote myself much more cheerfully to giving thanks: the renovated liturgy of Protestantism with the more noticeable insertion of the Christian drama into each worship—confession of sins, reception of pardon, joy of salvation —comes partly from you, partly from the Anglicans. In the same way, more frequent communion, and an architecture which ceases to put in the center of the Church a pulpit, replacing it with the communion rail and a cross, are derived from the neighborly contacts which have been bettered. In the measure in which tension diminishes, a fruitful communication is established. You will be surprised, no doubt, to find in my library Bossuet next to Calvin, Père Lagrange next to Frederic Godet, the Missal next to my Genevese liturgy. "Examine all things, and retain what is good." A salutary examination, the only fruitful one which is stranger to adulation as well as to abdication is born in a climate of reciprocal esteem.

I rejoice to know your opinion on the future relations of Catholicism with the rest of the Christian world; and I beg, dear Canon, that you will accept my expression of deferential and fraternal sentiments in our Lord.

JEAN RILLIET

22.

Reverend and dear Pastor,
On several occasions already we have spoken of ecumenism and have taken the resolution to explain ourselves on this

subject. You have done it in a very clear, forceful manner in your last letter and I would wish, in turn, to translate the Catholic feeling on the question.

The problem of ecumenism for us is nothing else than that of the reunion of the Churches. Under this different name, it is as ancient as the Church itself. From all time, there have come forth schisms, secessions and heresies. St. Paul declared that it is a necessary thing: "*Oportet haereses esse—* It is necessary to have heresies," and he gave the reason for it: "in order that those who resist the test may be manifest among you" (I Cor. 11:19). It is one of the difficulties wished for, or at least permitted, by God to serve as a test of the firmness and clarity of Faith. In the act of bringing people together, as we have tried, even here, there cannot be but profit for sincere Faith, which takes stock, so to speak, of its proofs and its riches, and which makes its position firm.

It is not less true that heresies are infinitely regrettable, when they last, when they cannot be reabsorbed, when they hurt in a too prolonged fashion the unity of the Church of Christ.

The unity of the Church! I have just written the essential word. There is in ecumenism a profound truth—that it is necessary to tend towards unity, that it must work in the sense of unity, that it is necessary with utmost speed and with all the means that God places at our disposal to come back to unity.

Here, simple reason is in harmony with faith. Simple reason tells us that Christianity loses its power in the face of growing impiety by its divisions; that it is time to present a common front in the presence of the adversary; that the responsibility of Christianity is plighted here, for it is a question of the highest interest of humanity.

Faith speaks still higher than reason in this domain.

It tells us that Jesus Christ wanted unity, that he imposed on us an imperious obligation, and that we lack love and fidelity towards Him when we draw profit from our divisions!

How can we forget the pathetic accents with which the "Good Shepherd" spoke of unity!

"I give my life for my sheep, and I have other sheep who are not of the fold; them also I must bring, and they will hear my voice, *and there will be only one flock and one Shepherd . . .*" (John 10:16).

How, especially, could we not be upset by the supreme prayer of Christ, not only for the present unity of His apostles, but for the future unity of generations instructed by them; that is, for the unity of the actual Church.

"But it is not only for these that I pray; it is also for *those who will believe in me because of my word,*"—it is indeed, then, for us Christians of the twentieth century—*"in order that all be one,* as thou, Father, thou art in me and I in thee, in order that they also be one in us, that the world believe that it is *thou who hast sent me.* For me, *the glory which* thou hast given me, I have given it to them in order that they may be one as we are one: I in them and thou in me, in order that they may be consumed in unity, that the world may know that thou hast sent me and that thou hast loved them as *thou hast loved me.*" (John 17: 20–23.)

Behold then the unity wished by Jesus Christ! What could He say more forcefully? What kind of unity could He propose which was more complete and perfect than the unity that He has with His Father?

Ah! how could we see even the shadow of such a unity in the praiseworthy but powerless efforts of ecumenism that have been shown up to now? Did Jesus Christ wish a federation of divergent Churches? Did He wish for an agreement, no matter what, based on "reciprocal concessions," as is written ordinarily? Is that the unity of the Father and the Son?

Kindly understand here the point of the Catholic position; we consider that the unity wished by Jesus Christ exists, that it has never ceased to exist in the bosom of the Church. There is among us an intimate unity, total, indefectible, a unity in the Faith, a unity in discipline, a unity in hierarchy, a unity in the communion of saints, as I said in my last letter. We desire nothing more ardently than the reunion of the Churches; but it is impossible that the Catholic Church show herself unfaithful to her divine mission by renouncing the unity which is hers in order to negotiate the conditions of a false unity, in the bosom of which each Church would remain what it is.

We are asked: "Why this haughtiness? Can wrongs not be admitted? There have been wrongs on both sides; we recognize ours and we deplore them; let the Catholic Church do the same, and a big step will be made in the direction of unity."

We reply: "Our haughtiness is not based on ourselves; and it is not a human haughtiness. Our haughtiness is Jesus Christ, and we cannot renounce Him. But if we were to admit against every evidence that our divine Founder did not provide for the future of revealed truth in an undulating and changing world, that He had abandoned His work to the discussions of men—and this about a sacred book—that He was powerless in the face of the inevitable "variations" of the human soul down through the ages, that He did not know in advance the hazards to which His doctrine would be exposed through the crises renewed without cease—the crises of Gnosticism, of Arianism, of Donatism, of Nestorianism, of Eutychianism, of Monothelism, of Protestantism, of Rationalist unbelief, of Marxism, and so forth—if we were to admit that, we would be unworthy of Him, we would lower Him to the human level, we would deny His divinity. He would no longer be for us the *only* One. He would no longer be the Saviour!

We could say with Tertullian addressing Marcio: "Spare the sole Hope of the universe!" Let us not touch, let us never touch the only Hope of the entire universe! We believe, on the contrary, that God is Love; that in His love He sent His only Son to redeem and to save us; that His only Son, acting in God, founded an infallible and indefectible Church, a hierarchical Church, of which the successor of Peter is the head in His name; and that He entrusted to that Church the intangible deposit of liberating truths, of dogmas of salvation. We have not the right to change an iota of this sacred deposit. "*Depositum custodi*—Guard the deposit," said St. Paul. We have not the right to admit into the unity of the Church those who have rejected any particle of this sacred deposit. Truth is one, or it is not at all. It is on the subject of truth that it is fitting to repeat that old adage: "*Bonum ex integra causa, malum ex quocunque defectu*—Good from the whole, evil from any defect." Truth does not suffer retrenchments, nor lessenings, nor bargainings, nor "reciprocal concessions." It is not of the domain of the relative, but very much of the absolute. The Christian religion may not be confused with a human doctrine, and may not be made an object of contradictory discussions, as is done in politics, in parliamentary assemblies.

That, too, is why we cannot admit the distinction between fundamental truths and secondary truths. Evidently the amputation of a finger is less harmful than that of a leg; and that of a leg preferable to corporal death. But, in the spiritual domain, everything is divine. All our dogmas are clear to us. They are not in the least a weight for us, no more than a diamond necklace is a weight for a princess. Our dogmas are our treasure. There is in each of them a power of life and love. We would not renounce, even at the price of life, the more recent pronouncements: the Immaculate Conception of the Virgin and her glorious Assumption. You cannot be unaware, dear Reverend Pastor, that this year, 1954, was proclaimed a Marian Year, by reason of the centenary of the proclamation of the dogma of the Immaculate Conception of Mary. This centenary has been marked, through all Catholicity, by festivities which, I can tell you, were not purely exterior. On the contrary, they gave rise to profound studies, to intense prayers, and to admirable acts of individual as well as collective piety. If, in the course of this exchange of letters with you, I have not been able to set forth the deep reasons of our Catholic Faith on the subject of dogmas which separate us and which you enumerated in one or the other of your letters, I would not wish to give the impression that I would have the least doubt about the legitimacy of our Catholic positions: the cult of the saints and, in particular, that of the Virgin; faith in purgatory and especially in the Real Presence in the Eucharist; faith in the Holy Sacrifice of the Mass; faith in the power of the keys in Sacramental confession.

In a word, the greatest service that the Catholic Church can render to Christianity and humanity is to remain herself and to follow her path, since it has been traced for her by the Holy Spirit himself. It is the case of repeating with Péguy: "Our allegiances are citadels!"

What about your wrongs, one will say, do you not want to recognize them? Most certainly we recognize them and very humbly. I have acknowledged them in one of my preceding letters, even citing the declaration of Pope Paul IV on this matter. Our wrongs are, nevertheless, the same! And they consist in this, that we are *not holy enough.* We do not live our dogmas, our Faith, our certitudes intensely enough! We do not reply enough to the infinite love with which we have been favored, and which urges us from every direction: *"Caritas Christi urget nos—*The charity of Christ urges us on." We descend too easily and too frequently from the Christian plane to the human plane, and oftentimes even lower! We do not remember enough the words of Christ: "Remain in my love! . . . If anyone loves me . . . my Father will also love him and we shall come in him, and we shall make our abode in him!" If we were habitually and lovingly attentive to this presence of the Holy Trinity in us by grace, in short, if we were to live a life of prayer, then the riches of our Church would shine forth more brillantly before the eyes of all, and especially we would obtain, without doubt, by our fervent prayers that God finally realize through us, with us, and in us, that glorious unity of the One Holy (*Una Sancta*), which is the moving dream of ecumenism, as you have described it in your letter.

To come to a more practical examination of the situation, I believe that one can define the hopes of the Catholic Church in the following manner. However, what I am going to say is personal. It is a spiritual point of view.

Non-Catholic Churches are not all equally distant from us. It seems possible with divine grace to attain, in the first place, a reconciliation of the Oriental Orthodox Churches and ourselves. They admit practically everything we admit. In the past there have already been two reunions of our Churches, the first in 1274 and the second in 1439. Between us there is nothing but prejudices sharpened by the years, racial oppositions, practices up to this point insurmountable. Alas! even here, one sees the whole difficulty of realizing the unity wanted by our Lord.

In the second place, an accord between the Catholic Church and the Episcopalian Churches, or at least with what is called the High Church, in the bosom of Anglicanism, should no longer be an inconsistent dream. I do not know whether Joseph de Maistre made a sure historical conjecture in writing, towards the end of his admirable book on the papacy: "All seems to point to the fact that the English are destined to give momentum to the great religious movement which is underway, and which will be a sacred age in the annals of the human race. To be the first to reach the Light, among those who have abjured it, they have two inestimable advantages, of which they are not aware: for, by the happiest of contradictions, their religious system is at once both evidently false and evidently nearer to the truth."

A genius of the first order, Newman has traced out a route for them. His books remain and can continue to light the path. The primacy of the pope is no longer the subject of doubt for thousands of Anglican ministers. What is being prepared there? God knows, and our prayers do not cease to implore Him for our "separated brothers."

"Separated brothers"—this word which I have just written we now use for Protestants also, among whom you are, Reverend Pastor. That gives me the occasion to answer directly the question which you bring up: "Are we still, in your eyes, heretics?" And you write: "A separated brother is not a heretic."

Here, I am truly afraid to cause you a grave deception. Assuredly, the term "heretic" has taken, in the course of the ages, a sinister meaning. There was a time (a time which we deplore) when one could say that this term—I am going to write an atrocious thing—"smelt of burning." I shall not try to bring judgment on the different and changing attitudes of Catholic powers, as of the Protestant authorities against dissidents. Reverend dear Pastor, we no longer relish casting at each other's head the burning in effigy of the Inquisition, or the martyrs of Gorkum and those of Tyburn. Let us speak calmly and peaceably.

A heretic, according to the etymology of the word, is, then, one who is separated—nothing more, nothing less! We can speak as much as we wish of "separated brothers"; by the very fact that we use "separated," we cannot mean any other thing than "heretic brothers." But what I grant you, with all my heart, is that the hour has come when, in speaking these two words, it is necessary to place the emphasis on the second more than on the first. Heretic, certainly, we cannot deny it; but brothers, and that is the meaning of the title which we have adopted for the book which will make known our correspondence: *Catholics and Protestants—Separated Brothers.*

Brothers, none the less. In this "none the less" there sounds a regret; one can detect a sigh! Yes, brothers, none the less; but not brothers as we should be, as Jesus wanted it, as His only Church, the One and Holy (*Una Sancta*), desires it.

On the other hand, you ask my ideas about the exercise of freedom of worship in Spain and in Colombia. On this point, I must disclaim all competence. One cannot give reasonable opinions on what one does not know. I am a subscriber to two reviews in the Spanish language: *Ecclesia* and *Incunable*. All I know is that both complain of the systematic calumnies of which Catholic Spain is the victim in Protestant countries. They state that Spanish Protestants—an imperceptible handful, according to them—have all the liberties which they can reasonably claim. I am not very sure that this is absolutely correct. However, I am not sure, either, that it is entirely false.

I do not believe, on the other hand, that it is truly useful to discuss here "liberty of thought" and "liberty of conscience." I would like to know what Jesus Christ thought on this point! One thing is liberty of thought and liberty of conscience in the political domain, in the bosom of our divided and aimless societies; another is liberty of thought and conscience in the face of divine Revelation! By what right could a man say to God, to Jesus Christ: "You have spoken; I believe it, and I tell you it is very good; but allow me, notwithstanding your word, my liberty of thought and my liberty of conscience"?

If by that we mean that God does not constrain us, that He wishes our free consent, that faith is not imposed, we are of one mind. If one means that the Word of God is not binding, that it does not create for us an obligation in conscience, to such a degree that error has as many rights as truth, we no longer are on the same path. It is just this discrimination, necessary between true and false, between good and evil, between God and Satan, that our popes, including Pius IX in the *Syllabus* (so many times commented on in this sense), have wanted to establish once and for all this thesis, while admitting hypothetically, the legitimacy and even the necessity of tolerance.

Enough discussion about all that. In short, there is a point where we are sure to meet, without deceiving ourselves. That is in fraternal charity. I hope I have never lacked it for one single instant in the course of our epistolary debates. There is a ritual practice in which we can and ought to unite our voices: it is in the prayer for unity! You with Bossuet in your library, Reverend dear Pastor . . . Let us reread, then, each of us, his magnificent sermon on unity. For myself, I repeat with him: "O Holy Roman Church, Mother of Churches and of all the faithful! Church chosen by God to unite His children in the same faith and in the same charity! We shall always adhere to unity from the bottom of our heart."

If it is necessary to end this correspondence with a prayer, I shall borrow the sentiments of our great St. Augustine. Speaking of the mystical wedding of Jesus Christ with His Church, he exclaimed in his sermon 138: "By the holiness of these nuptial ceremonies, I conjure you, love the Church, this Church; be of this Church; be this Church; love the Good Shepherd; pray for the dispersed sheep; that they may also come, that they may recognize the voice of the Shepherd, that there may be only one flock and one Shepherd."

And in his commentary on the Gospel of St. John he said: "Come, come, the dove calls you and she calls you moaning. O Catholics, my brothers, call by your sobs, by your prayers, by your fasts, so that the dissidents discover your charity and the grief that you have at their absence! May your invitation come to each of them, saying: 'Come, come. Have no fear. Come, and you will rejoice for coming. Come to the dove to whom it has been said: "One is my dove". . . Come to her, come . . .'" (*In Joan.*, Tract VI, 15).

Kindly accept, Reverend and dear Pastor, my very respectful and fraternal sentiments in our Lord.

L. CRISTIANI

XII

† / †

Separated Brothers

23.

Dear Canon Cristiani,

Your reflections on ecumenism reached me in the Grisons, where the vacations have been a relief from the stifling heat of Zurich. For a month now we have corresponded in an active manner, and our letters express clearly the divergent positions of our two Churches as we confront the problem of unity.

The Sunday before my departure while on my way to preach in the tiny chapel at Baden where the Swiss French Protestants assemble for divine worship, I passed in front of the Liebfrauenkirch (Church of the Virgin), the huge Catholic Church in Italian style. Under the porch, young people were chatting while waiting to enter the holy place. Through the wide open doors I perceived beyond the packed nave, a priest bent low before the altar. Our correspondence ran through my head. This sight, quickly registered, blended with it, as I went down the steps four at a time on my way to the station; and it followed me into the tiny church where I was to officiate a little later in the morning. That man, like me, is celebrating Christ the Saviour, I thought. The faithful assembled at the foot of the pulpit where I read the words of God raise to the Father the same hymns which intersperse the Mass:

> From the depths I cry to thee,
> O Lord, in my distress;
> Hear my voice, listen to me,
> Take away my sorrow.
> Before thee, I cannot stand
> If thou rememberest
> The sin which oppresses me.

Is not this, under another form, the *Kyrie Eleison?* And that cry of confidence and joy after the words of grace correspond to the *Gloria*, do they not?

> Glory to God, our Creator,
> Glory to Jesus, our Redeemer,
> Glory to the Spirit, our Consoler,
> Alleluia! Alleluia! Alleluia!

This is unity of Faith! Transubstantiation may be opposed to our symbolism; infallibility, to our acute sentiment of fallibility; the hierarchy, to our ecclesiastical republicanism; the role which you attribute to the saints and to the Virgin, to our persuasion that the merciful Christ receives each one of us directly. These important divergences do not supress the common faith in the Father, the Son, and the Holy Spirit.

The state of being exposed to error is peculiar to human nature. God does not fear liberty absolutely, since He made Adam capable of choosing good or evil. Jesus Christ, who bore Judas so long and allowed Peter to deny Him, admits also for his disciples the possibility of a gradual progress. The exercise of liberty in the face of truth is not to be confused with the decision of a chess player or a bridge player.

It involves an existence where each one, in seeking God, seeks himself. Freedom is I, it is my life, my reality as a man receiving into himself, little by little, the light which God sends to him. I come to certitude only through liberty; and yet it is not I who create truth. It is a revelation which dissolves the darkness—a miracle of grace. I can only receive the Gospel, the word of life; and yet, it is I who assimilate it and who teach it in turn. I understand that it irritates one to see the divine thus entrusted to man. God, the Omnipotent One, is the Author of that mystery which Alexander Vinet tried to explain in a well-known remark: "Truth without the search for Truth is only half of the truth." This paradoxical statement expresses a solid aspect of our spiritual position. A truth well-cooked—allow me this expression—is no longer a truth; the truth penetrates us through the jolts of selfishness and pride which yield slowly. "And you, will you also go away?" (John 6:67.) Do you think that the actual believer can understand the form of the sorrowful question posed by Christ to His disciples? An ecclesiastical system which claims to give to the Christian of the twentieth century what the Christian of the first century did not possess, troubles me.

You refuse to distinguish between fundamental and secondary truths. Protestantism reached its present position on this point only after a slow process. For one hundred and fifty years Geneva obliged its pastors to teach the predestination of Calvin. The quarrels and the divisions born of this dogmaticism led us to detest, little by little, the pretensions of punctilious theology. The Anglican Church goes still further in this matter and accepts the juxtaposition of Low Church parishes (very Protestant) and High Church (nearer to Catholicism). Canon Rawlinson recalls in a remarkable little volume, *The Church of England and the Church of Christ*, two judgments, which, in the years 1850 and 1871, on points as delicate as baptism and the Lord's Supper, maintained alternately the right for some to be symbolists and for others to be realists, their belonging to the Church of England not being contested (*op. cit.*, edit. of 1930, p. 82). The scale of religious nuances from Evangelicals to Anglo-Catholics in the interior of Anglicanism is, as a consequence, extraordinarily wide.

"*In necessariis unitas*—in necessary matters, unity." Does not the art of unity consist in limiting very strictly what is truly necessary to salvation? Thought is indispensable to life, and each one ought to think out his Faith; but he who, in the service of Jesus Christ, follows another route than mine merits my affection and esteem. I must offer him my hand even if his itinerary admits of useless detours. It was on the basis of this conviction that Soederblom convoked the Catholic Church to the ecumenical reunion of Stockholm, and that his successors imitated him without success. Is *he* truly the heretic, the one "separated" from the other, if he should invite in the name of Christ and receive the answer "No"? Is *he* not the heretic who separates himself because he believes that he is right all along the line? It is with sorrow that I write these words. "*Amicus Plato, magis amica veritas*— Plato is dear; Truth dearer."

May God grant that one day even on the ecclesiastical plane we may conclude in another fashion. Let us not forget in the meanwhile that, as long as we go our separate ways through the forest trees of doctrines and rituals, we shall step forth, one day, at the outskirts of the forest, looking towards the same horizon. "Then," says Saint Paul, "we shall see face to face . . . then I shall know as I have been known" (I Cor. 12:9–12).

Kindly accept, dear Canon, my sentiments of fidelity and deferential friendship.

Your brother in Christ,
JEAN RILLIET

24.

Reverend and dear Pastor,

In agreeing to exchange letters, we made a promise to clarify firstly what unites us, and secondly what separates us. Has our success been complete in the fulfillment of the task we assigned ourselves? I would hardly dare to be convinced of it.

Without doubt we have numerous and importants points in common. Yet between us there remain essential and irreducible differences. To have put them in focus is a worthwhile accomplishment. In this, my last letter, I would like to try and draw them still closer together, if possible. Truthfully I do not see things exactly as you in what concerns our differences.

If I understand your terminology clearly, this point—unmistakably clear—would separate us: that you like liberty, and that we do not; that you place the search for truth on the same plane as truth itself, whereas we like it (according to you) "all well-cooked."

I do not know why a text of St. Paul from his second letter to the Corinthians (11:22) spontaneously comes to my memory while reading your letter (like you, in fact, I have the habit of thinking "biblically" in everything): "I am speaking foolishly," cried out the apostle. "Are they Hebrews? So am I! Are they Israelites? So am I!"

For myself, I keep on saying: "They love liberty! So do I! They love the search for truth! So do I!" Here I speak foolishly, as a man: *More than they!*

Freedom is not, perhaps, the greatest gift of God to man, but it is the gift without which all others are valueless. We fail to understand how Luther, and then Calvin, could admit that Faith comes to us *without effort on our part*—that is, to the predestined alone—and that it justifies us and saves us without our *free* consent. Liberty in us is the very likeness of God. Without freedom there is no true faith. What is more serious, without liberty there is no possible love. What is a constrained love, a forced love, a non-free love? The love which He wanted from us was so costly that God gave us liberty to make it possible, despite the terrible risks that it permits, since it exposes the creature—angel or man—to a choice of rebellion and hatred through love of a false independence. Do not say, then—never say!—that we deny liberty, that we love it less than you. The truth is that liberty for us is not an end in itself, but the indispensable means of reaching the end which is love and service of God.

Likewise, we cannot allow it to be said that for us search for truth is reduced to a flicker, or even completely extinguished! Certain possession of the truth is, on the contrary, the most powerful stimulant for research, we think. Why is that? Because truth is a joy, a richness, an intoxicating treasure. One has never finished exploring it, digging deep for it, meditating on it, making an exhaustive study of it, and nourishing oneself on it. I would say right now that the supreme end for us—as for you, I suppose—is to love and serve God. Yet the love of God is a daily growth. St. John of the Cross, the prince of mystics, has spoken these marvelous words: "The health of the soul is love of God." He enumerates ten degrees of what he names "the secret stairway of love." The first is a detachment from earthly things and a desire of God. The second is *search for God*. Beyond that research, so dear to your great Vinet, there remain eight other degrees to mount: work for God, suffering for God, burning need of God, flight towards God, the kiss of God, mystical union with God, and so on. That ends only in heaven. Even if one finds all that too obscure, it is not evident that the possession of the Bible dispenses us from the study of the Bible; the community of thought with the Fathers, with the Councils, with the great Doctors and writers of the Church is one more reason for consecrating one's entire life—nay, it would take several lives!—to the study of the Bible, of the Fathers and the Doctors, without speaking of the saints!

If the difference between us, then, does not come from love of liberty, which is equal in both of us, nor from the passion for research, which is not less in us than in you, whence does it come?

I have already pointed out and I repeat in conclusion: what separates us is the concept which we both have of *unity in truth*. To speak more exactly, it is the profound exigence of our soul towards divine truth. We cannot admit in the Holy Spirit the least indifference between "Yes" and "No," between truth and error, between good and evil. Divine truth is an absolute. We have no right to detach one least particle from it, or divert the least emanation of it. You ask why the Catholic Church refuses to distinguish between fundamental and secondary truths. Quite simply because it does not belong to the human mind to make such a distinction with regard to revealed truths. You yourselves, as Protestants, have not been able to establish the distinction with certitude. What was fundamental for some, was secondary for others. What was more fundamental for Luther, and especially for Calvin, than the dogma of predestination? Yet you have rejected it, and you have done well. Many times I have thought of the indignation Calvin would feel if, returning among you, he should see that you had abandoned what he considered the central pillar of his doctrine. With what severity would he repeat that all the objections of human reason against this necessary dogma are only the "grunts of pigs"—his very words in *Christian Institution*.

Yet the wise reason which forbids us as Catholics the least concession in dogmatic matters can be worded as follows.

Since the departure of our Divine Founder, the Church has not ceased to discharge her responsibility in the name of Jesus Christ concerning dogmas confided to her guardianship. Suppose—a thing which is absurd and unthinkable in our eyes—that the Church abandons one only of His teachings or sets aside a single anathema with which she has struck out at error, she thus avows her fallibility. For you, that is nothing; it is an act of simple admission of human fragility: "*Errare humanum est*—To err is human." For us, it is truly another thing! It is the denial of the guaranty given by Jesus Christ. It is the disavowal of the promise which He made to His Church to assist her through the Holy Spirit forever. It is the crumbling of confidence which we have placed in our Saviour by thinking and professing that He did not come to let us wander about in the darkness and grope about in the night. Finally, it is a way of slighting His infinite love, of slighting Divine Providence, which, according to us, watches with infinitely more care over souls than over the stars of the firmament. On the ecumenical question, the risks are not the same for us as for you. One renunciation alone, and all crumbles—that is what is at stake for us! We would jeopardize our whole spiritual fortune by a single false move. For you, on the contrary—it seems to me—a variation, more or less, has not the same importance!

What shall we retain from this whole debate? This: that the thirst for unity ought to continue to devour us, that we ought to pray incessantly that our common Master unite His sheep in the same fold, that we ought to have confidence in the words which He spoke: "Ask, and you shall receive; knock, and it shall be opened unto you; search, and you shall find!" May He soon grant that most desirable grace—the union of the Churches around the successor of St. Peter!

Kindly accept, dear Pastor, my sentiments of deep affection in our Lord.

L. CRISTIANI